CW00602566

LANDSCAPE
RECORD

PRESIDENT	John Song, scz@land-ex.com
EDITOR IN CHIEF	Stone Wu, stone.wu@archina.com
EDITORIAL DIRECTOR	Sophia Aniston, sophia@land-ex.com
	Mandy Lee, mandy@land-ex.com
EDITORS	Lola Meeker, lola@land-ex.com
	Jutta Connor, jutta@land-ex.com
	Jessica Cyrus, jessica@land-ex.com
WEB EDITOR	Charley Anderson, charley@land-ex.com
DESIGN AND PRODUCTION	Pauline Hathaway, pauline@land-ex.com
CONTRIBUTING ILLUSTRATOR	Laurence Lee, laurence@land-ex.com
CONTRIBUTING EDITORS	Jeremy Zou, Arthur Gao
ADVISORY COMMITTEE	Patrick Blanc, Thomas Balsley, Lars Schwartz Hansen,
	Nick Wilson, Ive Haugeland, Mário Fernandes
MARKETING DEPARTMENT	Allied Architecture&Urban Group
MARKETING DIRECTOR	Shirley Liu, shirley.liu@ela.cn
	(86 21) 5596-8582 fax: (86 21) 5596-7178
BUSINESS DEVELOPMENT	Crystal Liu, crystal.liu@ela.cn
	(86 21) 5596-7278 fax: (86 21) 5596-7178
MARKETING EDITOR	Joanna Li, joanna.li@ela.cn
DISTRIBUTION	David Du, mail@actrace.com
	949/612-9958
READER SERVICE	Charley Anderson, charley@land-ex.com

LANDSCAPE RECORD (ISSN 2325-3339) MARCH 2014. NO. 2. (ISBN 978-988-12969-0-0) PUBLISHED BIMONTHLY BY PROFESSION DESIGN PRESS CO., LTD, 14271 JEFFREY RD, SUITE 191, IRVINE, CA 92620. **COPYRIGHT:** TITLE® REG. IN U.S. PATENT OFFICE. COPYRIGHT© 2012 BY PROFESSION DESIGN PRESS CO., LTD. ALL RIGHTS RESERVED. WRITE REQUESTS (NO TELEPHONE REQUESTS) TO 14271 JEFFREY RD, SUITE 191, IRVINE, CA 92620; **WEB SITE:** LAND-EX.COM **ADVERTISING:** ADVERTISING@LAND-EX.COM. **SUBSCRIPTION:** RATES ARE AS FOLLOWS: U.S. AND POSSESSIONS $60; CANADA AND MEXICO $69 (PAYMENT IN U.S. CURRENCY, GST INCLUDED); SINGLE COPY PRICE $10; FOR FOREIGN $11. **SUBSCRIBER SERVICE:** 949/612-9958. E-MAIL: LAND-EX@LAND-EX.COM. **INQUIRIES AND SUBMISSIONS:** PROFESSION DESIGN PRESS CO., LTD, 14271 JEFFREY RD, SUITE 191, IRVINE, CA 92620. **BACK ISSUES:** CALL 949/612-9958, OR GO TO LAND-EX.COM. INFORMATION HAS BEEN OBTAINED BY PROFESSION DESIGN PRESS CO., LTD. FROM SOURCES BELIEVED TO BE RELIABLE. HOWEVER, BECAUSE OF THE POSSIBILITY OF HUMAN OR MECHANICAL ERROR BY OUR SOURCES, PROFESSION DESIGN PRESS CO., LTD. AND LANDSCAPE RECORD DO NOT GUARANTEE THE ACCURACY, ADEQUACY OR COMPLETENESS OF ANY INFORMATION AND ARE NOT RESPONSIBLE FOR ANY ERRORS OR OMISSIONS THERE IN OR FOR THE RESULTS TO BE OBTAINED FROM THE USE OF SUCH INFORMATION OR FOR ANY DAMAGES RESULTING THERE FROM.

LANDSCAPE
RECORD

61

03 2014

ON THE COVER: Children playing around the Active Edge, photo by 1:1 Landskab
THIS PAGE: The square's flintstone fragments are defined by two types of curved concrete borders, photo by David Dudzik and Mandaworks
LEFT: The concept – to merge the traditional skatepark with a typical recreational park, photo by EFFEKT & Mads Krabbe
RIGHT: Singular tree, photo by Pablo F. Díaz-Fierros

Far East Organization Children's Garden opens at Gardens by the Bay

The new Far East Organization Children's Garden opens at Singapore's Gardens by the Bay on 21st January 2014, designed by Grant Associates – the same UK landscape architects behind the Supertrees and masterplanners of the award-winning Bay South Garden.

A major new feature of the 54-hectare Bay South Garden, the Far East Organization Children's Garden will offer a one-hectare mix of play experiences for all ages, including water play, rainforest tree houses, ridge top trails and topiary pergola arches all in a special garden setting overlooking the Marina Reservoir.

Andrew Grant, director, Grant Associates said: "The Far East Organization Children's Garden at Gardens by the Bay will create play opportunities that are not found elsewhere in Singapore that connect children to nature via technology, art and horticulture."

Dr. Kiat W. Tan, CEO, Gardens by the Bay said: "Words cannot express how pleased we are to offer children a special play area in Gardens by the Bay. This Children's Garden is made possible by the strong support of Far East Organization, and cements our commitment to creating a People's Garden with a green legacy for our future generations."

Interlace, a playground seamlessly fitting in its surroundings

Carve completes a new playground for the residential project Interlace designed by OMA in Singapore that seamlessly fits in its surroundings.

The Interlace is a new residential typology, which breaks with the standard isolated, vertical apartment towers of Singapore. Thirty-one apartment blocks, each six-story tall and identical in length, are stacked in a hexagonal arrangement to form eight large open and permeable courtyards. Light and air flow through the architecture and surrounding landscape.

In one of the courtyards, Carve built the new playground. To play is to learn from mimicking each other. In few cases, this also applies to designing play. While most playgrounds are a contrast to their surroundings – in color, shape and activity – the new Interlace playground is the mini-version of the surrounding residences.

Four large containers are stacked on top of each other, each one rotated just like the residential backdrop. Inside the containers, various crawling, climbing and sliding elements create a maze-like structure with a variety of adventurous routes. The "closed" facade gives children the thrill of being invisible, while the perforations actually ensure looks both inside and outside. Additionally, the perforated facades allow for shading and a continuous wind breeze, creating a cool climate inside the boxes whilst additionally stretching the borders of the conception of inside-outside.

Burgess Park

Designer: LDA Design
Location: Southwark, London, UK

Southwark's Burgess Park is central to some of the most ambitious regeneration projects in the country including the redevelopment of the adjacent Aylesbury Estate. The Mayor's Office recognized the importance of the Park to the wider regeneration of the area and selected it as one of its Priority Parks, adding funding to that which was already on the table from the New Deal for Communities.

Burgess Park, one of South London's largest parks, reopened in 2012 following an £8 million transformation funded by Southwark Council, The Mayor of London and The Creation Trust (formerly Aylesbury NDC). The Park borders the Aylesbury Estate; arguably one of the most ambitious regeneration projects underway in London. It was identified early on that Burgess Park would be central to the success of the wider regeneration efforts since the 51 hectares of park is such a significant green space in a densely built-up area. Many of the surrounding residents have little access to private open space, so Burgess Park plays a vital part of community life, creating opportunities for social interaction within a diverse demographic.

MASTERPLAN

1. Fields and meadow
2. Lakes and shores
3. Natural play and landform
4. Food for free
5. Wooded areas
6. Wild area
7. Plaza
8. Adventure play
9. Play
10. Heart of the park
11. Cultural hub and lawns
12. Gardens
13. Existing habit
14. Viewing platforms
15. Sports hub
16. Gardens and lawn
17. Green fingers

1. Photomontage of the play area with the undulating floorscape as an embedded imaginative play element. The painted lines and colorful areas add to the playfulness of the design
2. Photomontage showing the sunken butterfly garden with the reinstated Grand Surrey Canal in the distance

Project name:
Burgess Park
Completion date:
September 2012
Site area:
51ha
Cost:
8 Million Pounds
Photographer:
Cannon Ivers, Robin Forster, Southwark Council

In 2009, LDA Design won a design competition for the Park and then worked closely with the community to deliver the proposals, reaching out to over 1,000 people. They were appointed to be the lead landscape architect and masterplanner to create an imaginative 21st-century design for Burgess Park. The principle of creating a more legible park was fundamental. Before the Second World War the area was a grid of residential streets and canal-side factories. Following bombing and then slum clearance, a park developed over many years and in an ad hoc fashion. The result was a green space that not only lacked coherence but also a sense of connection with the adjacent communities.

PARK USE
1. Plaza
2. Food for free
3. Wooded area
4. Fields and meadow
5. Natural play and landform
6. Wild area
7. Adventure play
8. Play
9. Heart of the park
10. Cultural hub and lawns
11. Gardens
12. Lake and shores
13. Sports hub
14. Existing habitat
15. Viewing platforms
16. Gardens and lawn

BIODIVERSITY

Activity lawn
Species-rich lawn
Seasonal flowering meadow / amenity grasses
Scrub and woodland
Marginal wetland planting to land bridge
Wetland / nesting island
Lake
Garden meadow / feature planting
Community growing area
Butterfly garden
Orchard
Existing habitat grasslands and copses

PATHS CIRCULATION

Canal walk – 7m width
Grand axis walk – 5m width
Park-wide circulation
"Soft" path circulation – self-bound gravel
Perimeter circuit path

Crucial to the success of the redesign was creating a park that is attractive, safe and accessible to a diverse range of user groups. The design team re-shaped the existing topography, some 90,000m³ of soil, to create well-connected footpaths and sight lines through the park. Bold new entrances provide a strong identity for Burgess Park and draw inspiration from the site's rich history. The topography was sculpted to make the park more usable and to create a sense of drama and rhythm as users move through the space. These dramatic landforms reach 7 meters in height and set up wonderful compositions, direct people through the park and provide elevated views of the ever-changing London skyline. Intrinsic to the landforms, are contemporary meadows and planting devised by leading plantsman James Hitchmough. The meadows imbue the park with seasonal color displays throughout the year, provide valuable habitat and create a spectacular displays admired by park users.

1. Elevation of the 6-meter-high landforms that give structure to the park. These landforms have been sown with specialist display meadows
2. View of the Great Lawn with the lake and fountains in the distance. The Great Lawn is defined by two sculpted landforms that reach up to 7m in height, providing opportunities to view the London Skyline and the events in the Great Lawn
3. Montage view showing the "twisting" landforms, providing generous space for relaxation overlooking the park. Entrances into the park are defined by the steep planted banks of the landforms
4. This image shows the display meadows in their first year of flower after sowing. A loose, matrix effect is achieved by creating meadows from seed

Before

The existing site plan shows the disparate footpaths and the park's lack of structure. Redundant roads from the days of industry can still be seen on site.

The photo shows the old entrance arrangement at Camberwell Road, which included a myriad of paving types, narrow footpaths and understated entrance opportunities, lacking any connection with the active tennis court within the park.

The photo shows the old entrance arrangement at Old Kent Road, which included a series of steps, disparate planting, dated metal work features and obscured site lines into the park.

The photo shows the site condition of the park before it was revitalized, including redundant roads, adhoc topography that cut off sight-lines into the park and limits the sense of direction or wayfinding opportunities throughout the park.

After

The phase I Revitalization Plan shows the "Big Moves" to create a strong and legible structure to the park. This included reshaping the topography, introducing a cohesive footpath network and creating permeability to the perimeter of the park. The plan also shows the ambitious extension of the lake.

The Revitalization project created a "linear plaza" with ample seating with ample seating to afford views in to the tennis court. The screen and archway signal the entrance into the park, projecting a strong identity and character. The "linear plaza" includes three sustainable rain gardens that capture surface water drainage and provide rich planting displays throughout the year. The archways will include a Legible London Midilith, which is currently being mapped and is due to be installed imminently.

The Revitalization project re-profiled the entrance to create visual permeability into the site and created a more welcome and accessible entrance into the park. The screen and archway clearly identify the entrance to the park and the screen is site specific showing the historic road and street pattern of the site before it was converted to a park. The screens are 13.5 meters long and 3 meters high.

This dramatic view is taken in the same location and shows the lake extension, the immediate connection with the wider park and the Grade II Listed St. George's church spire. This view is taken from the new bridge that crosses the lake and provides an excellent prospect of the Great Lawn and associated park activities.

The multi-million pound transformation also featured a range of facilities, including a new over-fives playground, a 5km fitness route, competition level BMX track and a purpose-built barbecue area. The existing lake was redesigned and expanded with two 12-meter-high water fountains, wetlands and a 90-meter bridge designed to create a value connection for residents to access the adjacent school.

LDA design has transformed the Park by creating a clear structure and by opening up sightlines where they previously did not exist. The new Park features improved entrances, new paths, a re-worked lake, a new play hub, a competition standard BMX track, horticultural meadows, and extensive tree planting.

1

2

3

4

5

1. Plan view of the play area showing a dynamic and fluid organizational structure with a series of play zones

2-5. Images of the play area showing the undulating floorscape, which encourages children to use their imagination and creativity when playing in the play space. The slide tunneling through the 6-meter-high mound is the main attraction of the play area. The central swale captures all surface water drainage

6. Image of the main entrance showing the sunken rain gardens and sculptural landform. The first phase of the Aylesbury Estate redevelopment can be seen in the background

7. Elevated view of the other main entrance showing the arch, screen and rain garden with clustered seating opportunities

8. Montage view showing the architectural screens used at both entrances, which were inspired by the 19th-century road layout of the site

9. View of the expanded lake with fountains and clustered seating. The existing lake was doubled in size and purpose-built fishing platforms were provided

10. A national standard BMX track was completed on site by LDA Design working with Clark and Kent Contractors

1. "The thread" with walking path
2. Cabin near the shared Gainsbourg Gardens

Garden Serge Gainsbourg

Designer: Agence Territoires
Location: Porte des Lilas, Paris, France

Acquiring new surfaces by covering the ring-highway is a unique chance to bring Paris back into contact with its suburbs. However, this is not simply a topic of filling up the space, of closing the gap, but much more of opening up an old frontier. Previously separated districts need to be connected; a new center needs to be created.

The history of the deep and large cut of the ancient fortification and today's ring-highway is translated by an open space: a luxury in one of Europe's most expensive cities.

1

Project name:
Garden Serge Gainsbourg
Completion date:
2011
Architect:
Matthieu Gelin & David Lafon
Architecte
Light designer:
Light Cibles
Structure/Economy/Fluids
Engineer:
Integral 4
Road engineer:
ATPI
Client:
Semavip (Mixed Investment
Company of Paris)
Site area:
24,000sqm
Photographer:
Nicolas Waltefaugle

Here it becomes a vast meadow which is connected to its history as well as to its geography by visual axis to distant and nearby landscapes. Along the principal path numerous activities bring people together: playgrounds, a sports field, sun decks, common gardens…

The project organizes the garden around a large open space in the center, matching the layout of the device. The vegetation is concentrated on both sides. The central space is dedicated to the lawn and the meadow is left free. The gardens are located along the axis that links the boulevard to the point of view. The pond in the center is the place to harvest rainwater in addition to a large underground tank. Thanks to the pond, the garden can be grown and shown, and develop a living environment. On each side, under the trees, lay the other functions of the garden (children's games, reading room, home of the gardeners…).

SITE PLAN

Atalaya Park

Designer: G&C Arquitectos
Location: Plaza Atalaya, Armintza, Lemoiz, Bizkaia, Spain

Armintza is a neighborhood in Lemoiz formed by a chaotic clumping of buildings. The city's planning had been mismanaged and, as a result, its growth had produced numerous obstacles to the flow of pedestrians and vehicles. What's more, Armintza had no available public space of any consequence and parking was both uncontrolled and random. The town hall held an urban design competition and this was the winning project.

Objective

The objective of the intervention was to give the town of Lemoiz a public space where they could hold outdoor activities like festivals and exhibitions which would add to their appeal as a tourist destination.

To create a true town square which was open to the sea, well-defined architecturally, and that was capable of uniting its surroundings while also making them more attractive and dynamic meant that buildings in the area that had fallen into disuse had to be demolished.

The proposal outlines the creation of an outdoor space surrounded by vegetation. The focal point of the design is a garden bench that snakes through to create a fluid, yet cozy space that connects the church to the harbor. Both trees and bushes enclose the area, making it a protected, integrated zone that visitors can enjoy at their leisure.

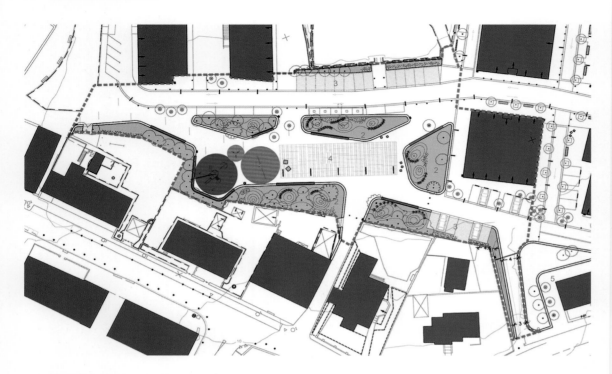

PLAN
1. Playground area
2. Green zones along the perimeter
3. Parking
4. Civic square
5. Church

Project name:
Atalaya Park
Completion date:
2011
Design team:
Marta González Cavia, Jorge
Cabrera Bartolomé, Martin
González Cavia
Developer:
Municipality of Lemoiz
Constructor:
UTE Construcciones Balzola-
Construcciones Azaceta
Site area:
4,000sqm
Use:
Playgrounds
Number of parking space:
24
Photographer:
G&C Arquitectos

A cobblestone "carpet" highlighted by a line of lamp posts, leads to a playground which is ringed along the perimeter by benches. To create the space and open up the view to the nearby harbor, an old, unused school was taken down. Sidewalks and paths were planned without changes in level to facilitate pedestrian mobility. The village church is incorporated into the new space by removing the existing retaining wall and creating a green slope that visually connects both spaces, restoring the original view of the chapel and making it the focus. Beside the church, a small area with views of the square is created and connected to the rest of the streets by stairs.

1. New view toward the church
2-3. Playground with rubber pavers
4. Children's playground

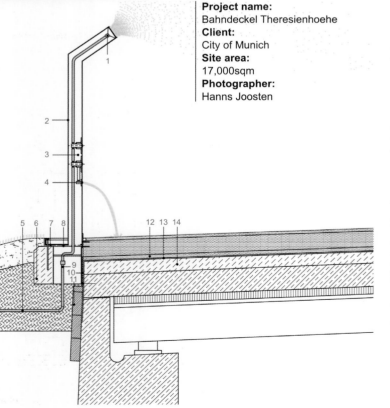

Project name:
Bahndeckel Theresienhoehe
Client:
City of Munich
Site area:
17,000sqm
Photographer:
Hanns Joosten

The "open space" project of the former trade fair area Theresienhoehe, in Munich includes the 300-meter-long and 50-meter-wide concrete plates above the railway connecting Munich to Rosenheim. The total area will be a new district of Munich offering office and residential buildings, shops, kindergardens and a school.

1. View from the lawn area to the play area
2. Sandbox play area
3. Lawn area with sitting bench
4. Vaulting horse

SECTION THROUGH FINE SPRAY AND FOOT SHOWER
1. Shower head
2. Steel frame shower, RAL 9005 jet black, 15 × 15cm, welded to the inner frame of the inspection cover
3. Shower button with valve timing gear, flush-mounted in steel frame
4. Water dispenser
5. Connection to the existing water supply
6. Inspection hatch on a concrete foundation, doweled
7. Inner hatch frame (cover), steel-checkered surface, RAL 9005 jet black, screwed to the outer hatch frame
8. Inspection hatch, 400 × 400 × 90mm, shut-off valve for water supply and water return facility for draining in winter
9. Flexible hose
10. Fleece-backed drainage matting, bonded to railway cover
11. Filter blocks
12. Poured asphalt, 4cm
13. Welded polymer bitumen sheet, 1cm
14. Blinding concrete, varying height

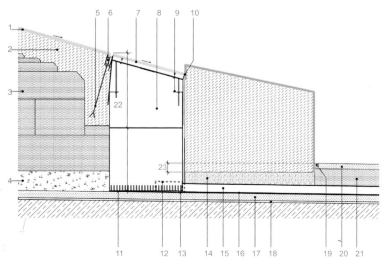

TYPICAL DETAIL OF INSPECTION TRAY IN THE GRASS MOUNDS
1. Astroturf, 13mm, fixed with restraining strips
2. Densely-textured lightweight concrete LC 16/18 with reinforcement
3. Modeling: Styrofoam blocks, rigid polystyrene foam
4. Profiling course: foam glass aggregate 10/50, min. 12cm (compacted)
5. Foundation anchor
6. Custom restraining strip type 4; screwed to the inspection tray
7. Cover plate: slotted, 13mm thick, Astroturf, bonded to grate with two-component adhesive
8. Base element of inspection tray, V2A stainless steel, 400 × 400mm, height 350mm, perforated base, open bottom, adjustable to adapt to contours
9. Top section, V2A stainless steel, height-adjustable, load category A15
10. Junction, 5cm beneath top edge of wall
11. Liquid plastic polymethyl acrylate sealant, fabric reinforced, 3mm

12. Longitudinal channel, 60 × 150 × 3mm
13. Flange, V2A stainless steel
14. Bedding of wall elements
15. Drainage pipe, V2A stainless steel, made of three box sections, each 50 × 80mm, 4mm wall thickness
16. Grout mortar bedding
17. Two-layer seal, 5cm; poured asphalt, 4cm
18. Welded polymer bitumen sheet, 1cm
19. Joint sealer, 20 × 20mm
20. Cover layer: asphalt concrete 0/8, 3cm
21. Base layer: insulation slab and poured asphalt
22. Variabel
23. 350mm

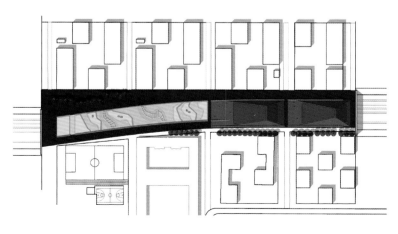

PLAYGROUND PLAN

1. Water-impervious layer: top layer of EPDM granules, 1cm; stopper coat; base layer of SBR granules, 3cm
2. Water-permeable layer: top layer of EPDM granules, 1cm; base layer of SBR granules, 3cm
3. Shaping of corner areas
4. Drainage inspection cover
5. Longitudinal channel, 60 × 150 × 3mm, V2A stainless steel
6. Soft fall zone, 2.50m
7. Trampoline
8. Small climbing dune
9. Crest line of railway cover
10. Large climbing dune

SECTION OF RAILWAY COVER CONSTRUCTION

A concrete cover over subterranean train tracks provides a connection between the newly constructed housing complexes south of Theresienhöhe in Munich. A new type of open space is conceived on this extraordinary site between Bavaria Park, Theresienwiese and West Park. The train tracks beneath the large concrete cover constituted the starting point for the project design developed in collaboration with Rosemarie Trockel and Catherine Venart. A series of play elements were installed on the cover, in a row as an allusion to the trains traveling beneath; this procession of containers transports material and, in a figurative sense, the powers of the imagination, just like a toy box.

Together with artist Rosemarie Trockel and architect Catherine Venart, the "Bahndeckel" is designed to be an important open space in this new area. The chaste and clear concept consists of an orange and green lane – a multifaceted urban space, connecting three landscape elements and combining different materials. A rubber-paved strip moves from one side to the center of the stretched-out space, and a lawn-strip comes from the other side. In the center a sand dune rises above the area which edge is subject to constant change due to permanent usage. The entire space is accessible from all sides. A low wall to sit on surrounds the area, turning into a higher supporting wall along the grass section. Along one side of this wall an over-dimensioned ball-net is spanned. In the background, accentuating pine trees are planted in large pots, providing shade with their crowns.

This newly developed site incorporates three materials that can also be identified as elements of landscape: a sports and playing area is made of rubberized tartan, a meadow is formed by a lawn and, between them, there is a large expanse of sand and gravel.

A pine grove accentuates the slightly curved north perimeter of the track. Along both sides of the open space green front-gardens connect the project with the adjacent housing. The landscape cover is a generous open area accessible from all sides which, on one hand links the residential areas on both sides by means of imagined movement but on the other hand, provides a soothing contrast to the density of the adjoining housing developments, and a sense of being faraway within an absurd locality.

This wide and open space stands in contrast to the dense urban structure of the adjacent buildings. With its many uses the "Bahndeckel" will become a new attractive urban square.

1. Detailed view of railway cover construction
2. Vaulting horse with playing kids
3. Soccer game on artificial lawn
4. Main climbing feature
5. Trampolins in play area

Leifsgade Square

Designer: Preben Skaarup Landskab | **Location:** Amager, Copenhagen, Denmark

Greenery

It has been important that the square should have more green appearance. A challenge when 2/3 of the square only is covered with only one meter soil as a result of the car park below.

The trees and plants are all planted in unbroken gravel beds. Along facades are planted crab apples and different climbing plants on espaliers. Around the street football area and the playground are planted acacia. All trees are standard to secure maximum transparency in eye level looking across the square.

To compensate for the missing underground surface all water from the middle of the square are led to the gravel beds for absorption.

Lighting

The whole square area light up from spots hanging from wires running across from facade to facade. On the masts which carry the wire are placed spots lighting up the nearest trees with orange and blue light. There are light in traffic cones and espalier.

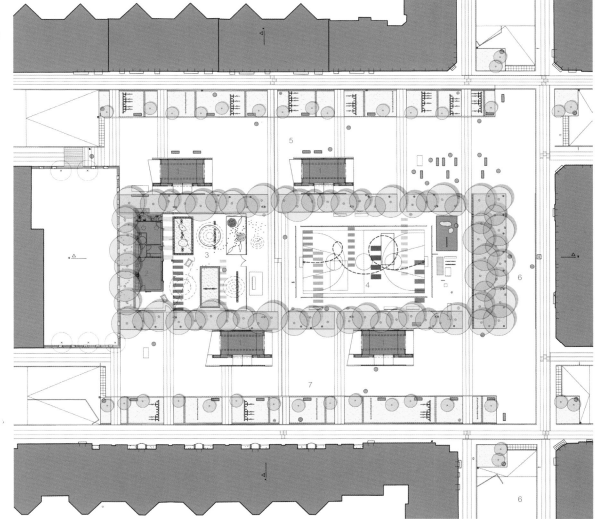

SITE PLAN
1. Elevator box
2. Pavilion
3. Playground
4. Playing field
5. Gunlogsgade
6. Leifsgade
7. Bergthorasgade

San Girolamo Urban Garden

Designer: bdfarchitetti | **Location:** Bari, Italy

The garden is located in the residential district of San Girolamo, on the northern coast of Bari, and it stands between its main crossing axis (San Girolamo street) and Nicola Costa street. The district of San Girolamo is a part of the city where, starting from the 1980s, were built many public and private housing constructions, but the residential program did not correspond to the realization of free public spaces. Actually the project tries to reflect the requirement of a new spirit of social sustainable urban space designing a garden that is also a square and that not only has the role of changing the skin of an empty space, but first of all to connect all the residential parts of the district.

1. Overview of the urban garden
2-3. View of the lights, trash can and basins

2

3

Through a participatory planning the project gave to citizens the opportunity to know the program and to participate directly in the development of the design process, so to foster tolerance, education, cultural diversity and social mix.

The project transforms a rough land into an open public space made of an "Apricena" stone surface with five big rectangular green basins on it, parallel and staggered one to each other, oriented like the opposite sporting area, which is ideally connected to them. The staggering produces an articulation of roads and small squares that increases the enjoyable spaces. The big basins are like strips of land that rise up from the horizontal and create, in their highest part, a concrete wall with an articulated section that becomes a bench system. The small squares appear alternatively at the internal part of the garden and along the street, in order to dissolve the limits with the surrounding space.

The design of the bench pays homage to the Spanish artist Jorge Oteiza's sculptures: made of painted sheet-steel, the bench has a concept based on its use in different positions. The seat has three places, two with a back and one free to permit turning toward the opposite direction, and the head of the back is bended so to make a shelf on which is possible to lean or put objects.

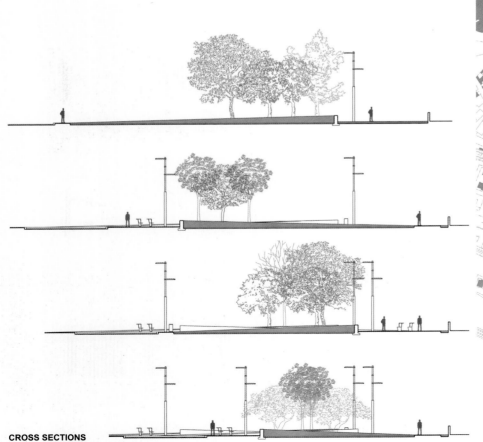

CROSS SECTIONS

SITUATION PLAN

Project name:
San Girolamo Urban Garden
Principal landscape architects:
Vincenzo P. Bagnato & Pasquale A. de Nicolo (bdfarchitetti)
With:
Massimiliano Fiore; Arriola&Fiol Arquitectes (Andreu Arriola & Carmen Fiol); Ricerca&Progetto (Nicola Martinelli)
Structure:
Filippo Surace

Systems:
Roberta Rana
Consultants:
A. Bernardoni (agronomy)
D. di Carne (geology)
Collaborator:
S. Micunco
Client:
Comune di Bari
Site area:
2,169sqm
Cost:
268,491.15 Euro

Photographer:
M. Cera
Awards:
Apulia Prize 2011 for Projects of Contemporary Architecture and Urbanism (Selected Project – Section Under 40); Giarch - Projects of Young Italian Architects 2011 (Selected Project); 27/37 - International Exhibition of Young Italian Architects Shanghai 2010 (Selected Project)

1. Five big rectangular green basins
2-3. Close shot of green basins and the lights

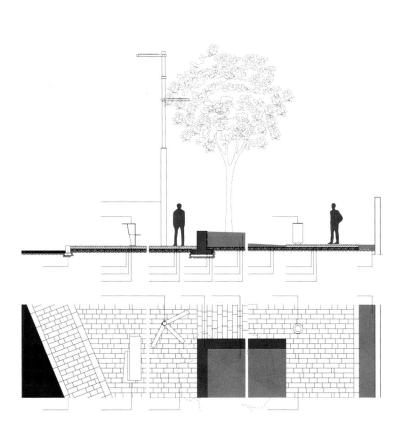

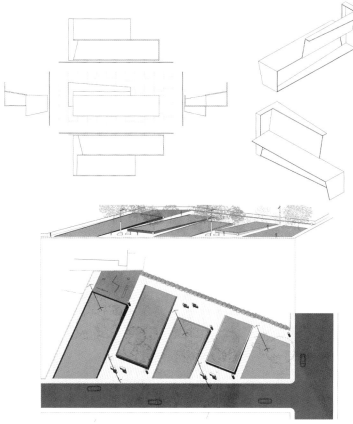

PLAN AND AXONOMETRIC VIEW

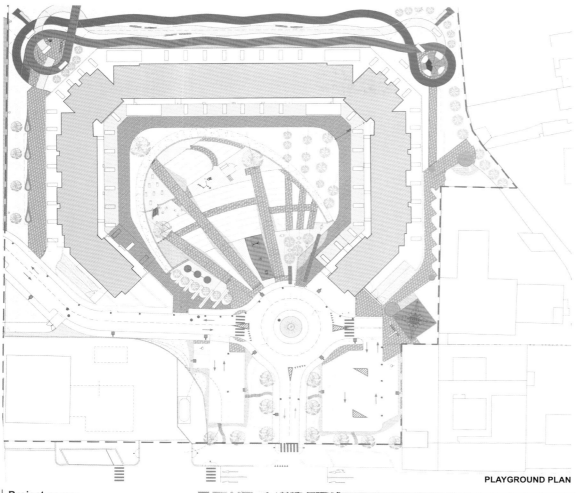

PLAYGROUND PLAN

The architects tried to develop a more dynamic and functional space that is easily accessible to bicycles and suitable for physical exercise. They focused on the involvement of the local community during the planning phase starting from primary school children, by developing a creative approach and raising awareness and respect for public areas. They choose trees and plants together with children, and the park was planned to obtain different shades of green, while adding a splash of colorful spots to the environment also in the winter season.

Design Process

Renovation projects, new urban décor solutions, children's playgrounds, usability projects and socialization-oriented projects, and a new lighting system: new life has been breathed into parks and gardens, while suburban and urban centers have been given a new role, saving them from urban decay.

Project name:
Casino Barolo Garden
Agronomist:
Marta Vitale, Stefano Fioravanzo & Guido Giorza
Budget:
2,960,000 Euro
Site area:
29,000sqm
Use:
Public gardens, playground, fitness area and urban vegetable (kitchen) garden
Photographer:
Marco Minari
Awards:
Premio la Città per il verde 2009 (Green City Award 2009)

1. Fitness
2. Bike track

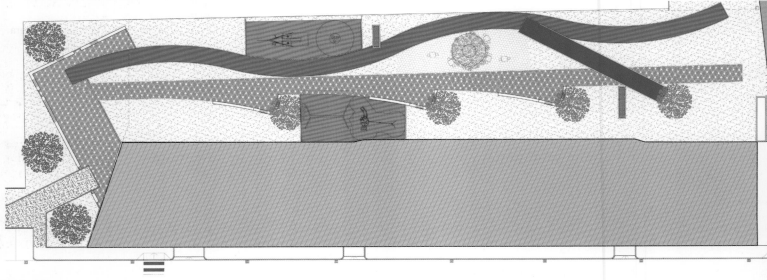

BIKE PATH

In this instance, the renovation plan concerns a large area, which extends over a floor surface of 29,000sqm and which includes parks and gardens, cycle lanes, fitness areas, playgrounds and other useful services, all served by a new lighting system. Overall a large area has been reclaimed: about 90 trees, 1,000 plants and 10,000 shrubs have been planted.

Lighting was part of this project. The architects chose the pencil-shaped light pole, which is totally different from traditional poles, and is the only one of its kind dedicated to children. Its shape is definitely more interesting to use in this recreational and colorful context. Light redesigns space, promotes usability and safety while saving energy.

The project ensuing from this approach is multi-stranded, and offers a variety of opportunities. For instance, vegetable gardens (or kitchen gardens) were created, which will be allocated to the locals, primarily to people on a low income, as a way to help reduce family expenditure.

Altessano road gardens are different from traditional public gardens, also in terms of urban furnishings. Color is used in abundance to differentiate pedestrian and cycle lanes; there are original concrete sofas, and unusually flower-shaped lighting fixtures installed on pencil-shaped light poles.

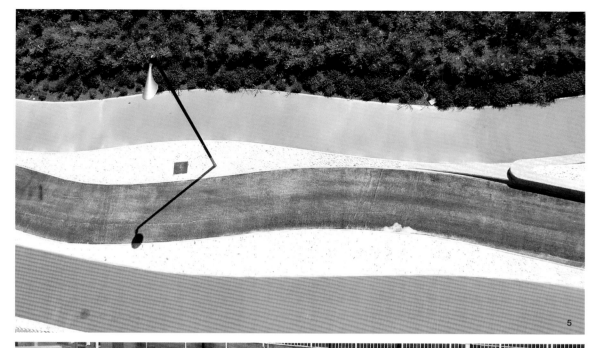

It is important to encourage people to go out at night, rather than let crime and vandalism take over. A new lighting system for green areas, bike lanes, and children's playgounds enhances the paths, projects cones of light in those areas where people can meet, and also emphasizes the most minute details like some species of plants and original seats.

Main Plants
- Trees: Cercidiphyllum japonicum purpureum, Cornus florida "rubra," Davidia involucrata, Gleditsia triacanthos "sunburnst," Populus tremula, Pyrus calleryana "Chanticleer," Clerodendrum trichotomu, Liriodendron tulipifera , Morus nigra, Prunus avium
- Shrub: Abelia grandiflora, Hibiscus syriacus "Blue Bird," Ligustrum ovalifolium texanum, Mahonia aquifolium "Apollo," Osmanthus x burkwoodii, Prunus laurocerasus "Otto Luyken," Spiraea japonica "shirobana," Spiraea bumalda, Syringa vulgaris, Viburnum tinus "Eve Price" Cotoneaster dammeri "Coral Beauty," Liriope muscari, Juniperus sabina tamaricifolia, Juniperusp pfitzeriana chinensis "blue and gold", Juniperus procumbens
- Grasses: Festuca glauca, Carex morrowii "Ice dance," Festuca "sea urchin," Miscanthus sinensis "Zebrinus"
- Bamboo: Sinarundinaria murielae, Phillostachis aurea, Phillostachis nigra

Materials of Construction
- Urban furniture: tables and benches in reinforced cast stone and in wood and steel, stainless steel pergola, steel canopy shade, benches and walls in red-colored deactivated concrete
- Fitness and playground furniture: hot-dip galvanized thin-walled iron tubes, polyamide
- Flooring: rubber floor, sport turf, regenerated porphyry cubes, colored resin, concrete blocks

1. Tettoia
2-3. Urban furniture
4. Children playground
5. Bike track
6. The vegetable kitchen garden huts

Elizabeth Caruthers Park

Designer: Hargreaves Associates, Inc.

Location: Portland, Oregon, USA

The South Waterfront Neighborhood Park links program to landscape typology with a focus on ecological experience with intermittent program nodes. This park will serve a new city-planned mixed use, sustainable high-rise development on a former industrial district along the Willamette River, just south of downtown Portland. The new development emphasizes sustainable practices through alternative transportation, LEED-certified buildings, clean energy production and integrated stormwater management. The South Waterfront Neighborhood Park contributes to the sustainability goals of the new urban neighborhood by treating stormwater on the site and attracting wildlife. The 0.8-hectare park will serve an estimated 5,000 residents plus another 5,000 commercial and institutional users of the vicinity.

The design of the park creates an overall structure with clear spatial divisions into three distinct landscape typologies. A loose program is nestled within the landscape typologies, emphasizing the integration of varied activities with a localized landscape experience. The park is composed of a Multi-Use Lawn and two ecological landscape typologies – the Urban Garden, and the Naturalized Landscape – that emphasize the wet gardens and native forests of the Pacific Northwest. The Naturalized Landscape abstracts the lush landscape of the Pacific Northwest with a dense forest

canopy punctuated by small clearings. Native plants including Western Red Cedar, Sword Fern and Oregon Grape create a woodland structure, while Columbine, Bleeding Heart, and Camass provide informal accents of seasonal color. As the entire site had been raised out of the floodplain for development purposes, the wet, undulating landscape form refigures the displaced riparian landscape of gulches and varied landforms in the park. Surface water collects across the park and infiltrates in four depressed water infiltration gardens, recharging the first flush of storm events on site and cleaning storm water that is eventually released into the Willamette River.

The infiltration gardens are also partially irrigated by overflow water from the interactive fountain in the Urban Garden, which keeps the gardens wet and contributes to the ecological conditions of the Pacific Northwest Lowland plantings. Clearings in the Naturalized Landscape feature an environmental artwork called Song Cycles, which creates soft chimes from the wind that passes through the site, making visitors aware of the environmental phenomena on site. Wood boardwalks wind

through the gently undulating forest, referencing the historic waterfront. The Naturalized Landscape and the Urban Garden have inverse spatial relationships. While the Naturalized Landscape is comprised of a dense canopy and small clearings, the Urban Garden section of the park features a highly textured ground plane punctuated by elliptical landscape islands. The landscape islands create nodes of programmed activated space, including

Project name:
Elizabeth Caruthers Park
Architects:
Boora Architects
Artists:
Doug Hollis, Margo Sawyer
Local landscape architects:
Lango Hansen Landscape Architects
Fountains:
Dan Euser Waterarchitecture

Site area:
approx. 0.8ha
Photographer:
Jason King

1. Grass with bench
2. Path
3. Overall view

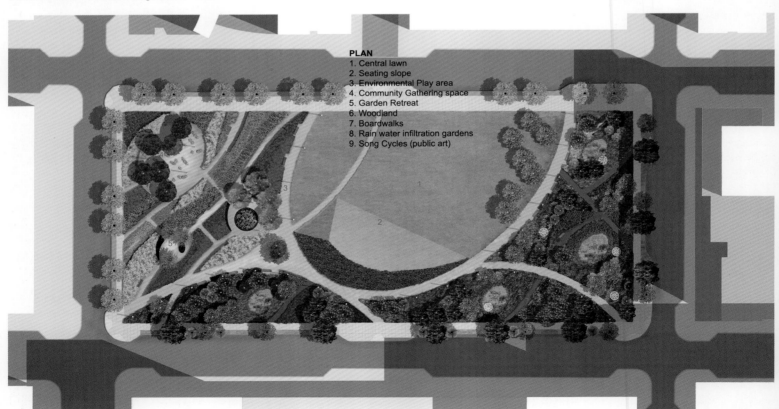

PLAN
1. Central lawn
2. Seating slope
3. Environmental Play area
4. Community Gathering space
5. Garden Retreat
6. Woodland
7. Boardwalks
8. Rain water infiltration gardens
9. Song Cycles (public art)

an Environmental Play area with an interactive fountain that evokes stepping stones in a stream, a Community Gathering area with moveable tables and chairs, and a Garden Retreat for quiet contemplation. The texture of the ground plane is created by sinuous mass plantings that can be read as a graphic from the surrounding high-rise buildings. The landscape islands provide a sheltered gathering space under a tall canopy of trees within the textured ground plane. The form of the planted areas and circulation system suggests the movement of water flowing across the site, weaving through the gardens as water would carve paths over a landscape. The plantings are four-season plants, emphasizing seasonal change and reinforcing the reading of environmental phenomena on the site.

The Multi-use Lawn allows for flexible lounging space and active recreation and event space for nearby residents. The added elevation of the seating slope on the Multi-use Lawn allows visitors to view the lower elevation of the Willamette River several blocks away, visually connecting the park to the waterfront. Because of frequent rainy weather in Portland, it was important to locate the lawn in the ideal microclimate on the sunny and protected side of the site.

Though a small site, richness is layered throughout the site with largely passive yet varied program, and a dedication to creating environmental meaning on the site. The park will be the primary gathering space for the neighborhood, with retail development activating adjacent ground floor edges, while at the same time providing an ecologically rich experience of place. The landscape typologies reference native ecologies and contribute to the overall performance of this new urban district. The infiltration gardens at the South Waterfront Neighborhood Park interface with the City's existing green stormwater infrastructure and create a network of small-scale stormwater interventions that act exponentially when taken as a whole.

3

Hundsund Community Center

Designer: Bjørbekk & Lindheim AS | **Location:** Oslo, Norway

Hundsund Center is built around a central pedestrian zone that is designed to pull together the fabric of the center and provide access to all the facilities. The new buildings for the junior high school, the nursery school, the sports grounds and the indoor swimming pool each have their own entrance from the precinct. Vehicles approach the precinct for loading and unloading at a roundabout at the beginning of the central zone.

PLAN
1. Central "community" street with water feature and artistic installations
2. Public swimming pool
3. Sport hall
4. Primary school and secondary school with playing area
5. "Activity string"
6. Outdoor sports area
7. Kindergarten with playing area
8. Arrival area for cars

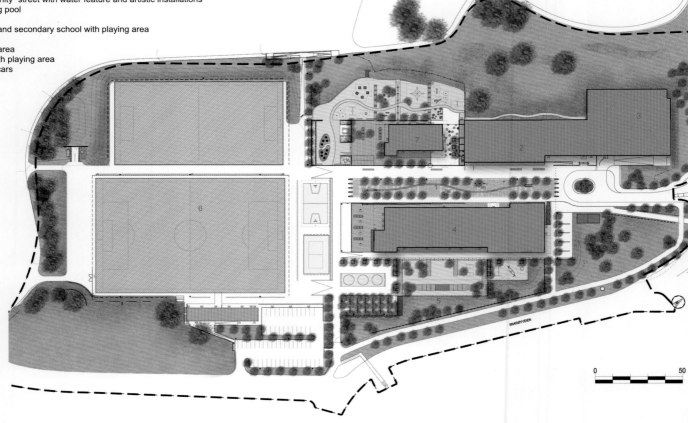

The area is designed to become a social meeting point for the new residents of Fornebu. The granite flooring of the central zone has water running in a curved gulley through it as a refreshing element.

The school and nursery school to the east and west of the precinct each have their own spacious outdoor areas. The buildings are surrounded by partly covered patios made of larch heartwood that open out to the south in large terraces with long tables and benches. Here children can participate in outdoors lesson and work on projects. The junior high school has a double-level outdoor activity area. On the lower level are a series of structures and a stage for performances, as well as roped units to encourage climbing, outdoor meeting places on the upper level. There are also three hollow half-

3

circles made of poured concrete for skating, biking, running and sliding. The outdoor area of the nursery school has a winding bike path moulded with ups and downs, a wooden pier, a water canal with a pump, a ladybug-inspired knoll covered in soft-fall safety grass, a village of five small wooden playhouses. There is also a little kitchen garden, willow shrubbery that provides hidey holes and a "Hundred Acre Wood" to play in.

There are astro-turf playing fields, an ice skating rink and basket and beach volleyball courts to the south of the precinct.

1. The end of water channel
2-3. The fountain
4. Roped units

5. Slide
6. A wooden pier
7. Hollow half-circles made of poured concrete for skating

Project name:
Hundsund Community Center
Architect:
div.A Arkitekter
Site area:
72,000sqm
Photographer:
Bjørbekk & Lindheim AS / Andreas Øverland
Awards:
2009 National Building Design Prize (Statens Byggeskikkpris) Nomination

4

5

6

7

Hermods Plats

Designer: Mandaworks | **Location:** Klagshamn, Malmö, Sweden

Task

Hermods Plats was planned by the municipality to become the central public space in the expanding village of Klagshamn, Sweden. To help bring identity and bind the village together, Hermods Plats was commissioned with the aim of creating a community square that minimized the presence of the site's existing barriers, invited local activity, and brought a stronger sense of community to the village.

Background

Klagshamn is located on the southern periphery of Malmö and is a portion of the Malmö Municipality. Klagshamn is surrounded by a beautiful cultural landscape and a variety of rich natural areas that help define Skåne's regional landscape. In the late 1800s, the village emerged as limestone began to be mined in the area. From the mining the community grew as a railway, small industry, hotels and schools emerged. When the quarry closed, village development stalled and the quarry was turned into a lake. In recent years the growth of Malmö and the Oresund Region have brought new interest in Klagshamn as a series of new urban developments have brought new residents, a new spatial structure, and a new life to the village on the edge of Malmö.

Statement from the Designers

A neighborhood square grown out of the site's movement patterns, geological history, and surrounding architectural qualities, Hermods Plats brings a new identity to the village of Klagshamn. Inspired by the fragmentary nature of the flintstone found in the surrounding landscape, the design connects across the bisecting street to form a unified square that prioritizes pedestrian flow and creates a cohesive design language. The resulting design creates a series of rooms, called fragments, which tie together the old village structure with the newly developed residential area.

Responding to their adjacent context, each fragment is defined through a series of curved concrete edges that vary in height and function. Within the square there are two types of concrete edges: one is a thin line in level with the floor surface that respects the site's lines of desire and the other is a thicker, elevated wall that supports in-situ seating areas, a jeu de boule play area, and elevated vegetation areas. Collectively the differentiated edges organize a selection of floor treatments and softscape materials that bring a strong design identity while also answering to the municipality's demand for adaptability over time.

Now open, the square has become a connective space that blends activity areas for young families with textured landscape elements, a local bus lane and sitting areas for neighborhood residents. The square's patchwork of hardscape elements have created an immediate identity to Klagshamn and the developing landscape of native grasses, pine trees and flintstone is only beginning to define the future rooms.

Project name:
Hermods Plats
Completion date:
2013
Design team:
Martin Arfalk, Nicholas Bigelow, Gregorio Chierici,
Max Haluzan, Ola Nielsen, Mike von Tiesenhausen
Consultant:
Vectura (Construction Documents), Malmö
Municipality
Client:
Malmö Municipality
Site area:
3,600sqm
Photographer:
David Dudzik and Mandaworks

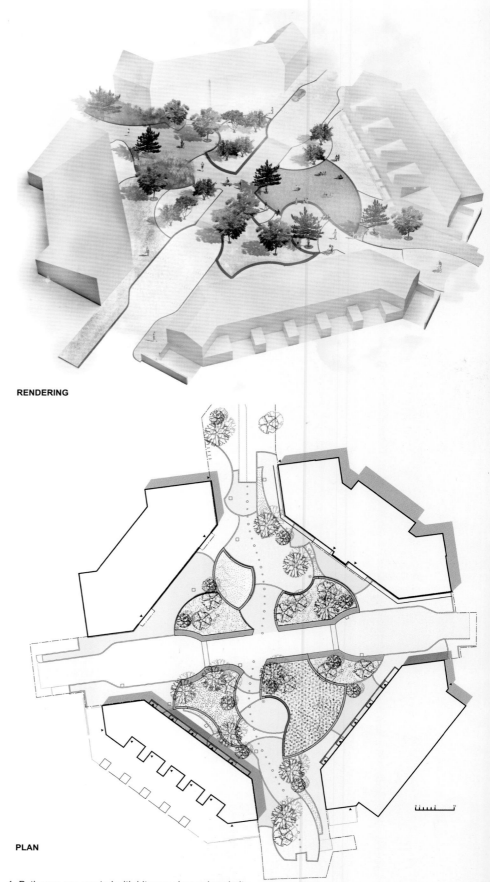

RENDERING

PLAN

Additional Information on the Design

A Connective Space
In the first discussions with the municipality a key challenge emerged: the square was at risk of being divided into two pieces by an existing east-west street bisecting the square. The street was planned to both provide vehicular access to the surrounding neighborhood and a bus stop on one of the city's bus lines. Mandaworks' design connects across the street in three ways. First, they prioritize the north-south pedestrian connection by lifting the street on level with the square to link the new development to the established village. Second, they integrate the street and the required bus lane into the flintstone-inspired pattern to create a cohesive sequence of spaces. Third, the square's rooms are positioned and designed to connect to the variety of design challenges within the site.

A Dynamic, Layered Square
The square's flintstone fragments are defined by curved concrete borders. The evocative concrete forms clearly reference the site's local geological history and the sharp shape of the local flintstone. The concrete is poured in place to give two types of edge conditions. One is a thin line (20cm) in level with the surface that is used to create visual depth, mark material variations, and allow for unbroken pedestrian movement. The second type is a thicker (50cm), elevated wall that slopes to define the square's rooms and surrounding planting beds. Together, these concrete edges guide movement patterns, create a visually layered landscape, and integrate seating into the square.

1. Pathways are created with bitumen-dressed asphalt
2. The square's flintstone fragments are defined by two types of curved concrete borders

Details Provide a Sense of Place & History

The design's details create a sense of place that links to both the history of the place and the new modern neighborhood. Within the flintstone-inspired pattern, pathways are created with bitumen dressed asphalt. The three-color variations pick on surrounding building material and create a dynamic and memorable floor in the face of budgetary constraints. Surrounding the pathways, three planting beds filled with flintstone express the tactile qualities of the local geology. Within the planting beds, concrete seats are designed to evoke tree stumps and mixed with native vegetation to remind visitor's of how Skåne's once forested landscape was harvested to create its current agricultural landscape. Other elements within the square have been developed from standard site furnishing in collaboration with Swedish manufacturing companies. Examples of the design team's collaboration include the unique details of the small flintstone chipping patterns on the air well lids for trees and two long curving benches that provide integrated seating places within the square.

SECTION

A Textured Green Space

Planting areas are integrated into the square to define the square's rooms. At eye level, the plant material consists of a variety of grasses, perennials and bulbs that are designed to bring texture and seasonal variation. Planting fragments range from growing a mix of tall grasses that define a room to limited plantings near the street to keep view lines open. The highest grasses (3m) are placed in a planting bed that is prepared for the future square fountain. The square's 33 trees are arranged in clusters with a few separated specimens. Collectively the species of Amur maple (Acer ginnala), Black Pine (Pinus nigra), Black Locust (Robinia pseudoacacia) and Sumac (Rhus typhina) will form a green roof over the square and bring a variety of textures and seasonal interest.

Light to Emphasize

The lighting plan uses projection lighting to highlight key design features in the square. The plan tries to emphasize the designs curving forms and programmed to create a night time dynamic. Collectively the light provides safety for all evening visitors, but the focused lighting helps create a striking atmosphere that accentuates the square's variety of materials, its unique forms, and vegetative qualities.

Adaptability for the Future

As the new neighborhood around Hermods Plats was recently built and its limited budget forced value engineering, the square's design team conceived it to adapt to potential changes in the neighborhood as it ages. The square responds to the adaptability of the architecture by setting aside areas for future cafes. Infrastructure for future improvements, such as the future square fountain, has been prepared. Additionally, the framework of concrete edges provides a structure for the neighborhood to incrementally change or add to the square's program or planting regimes as they make their community square their own.

1. One is a thin line (20cm) in level with the surface
2. The other is a thicker (50cm), elevated wall which supports the seating areas
3. View of the tree stumps
4. Visualization
5. These concrete edges guide movement patterns and create a visually layered landscape

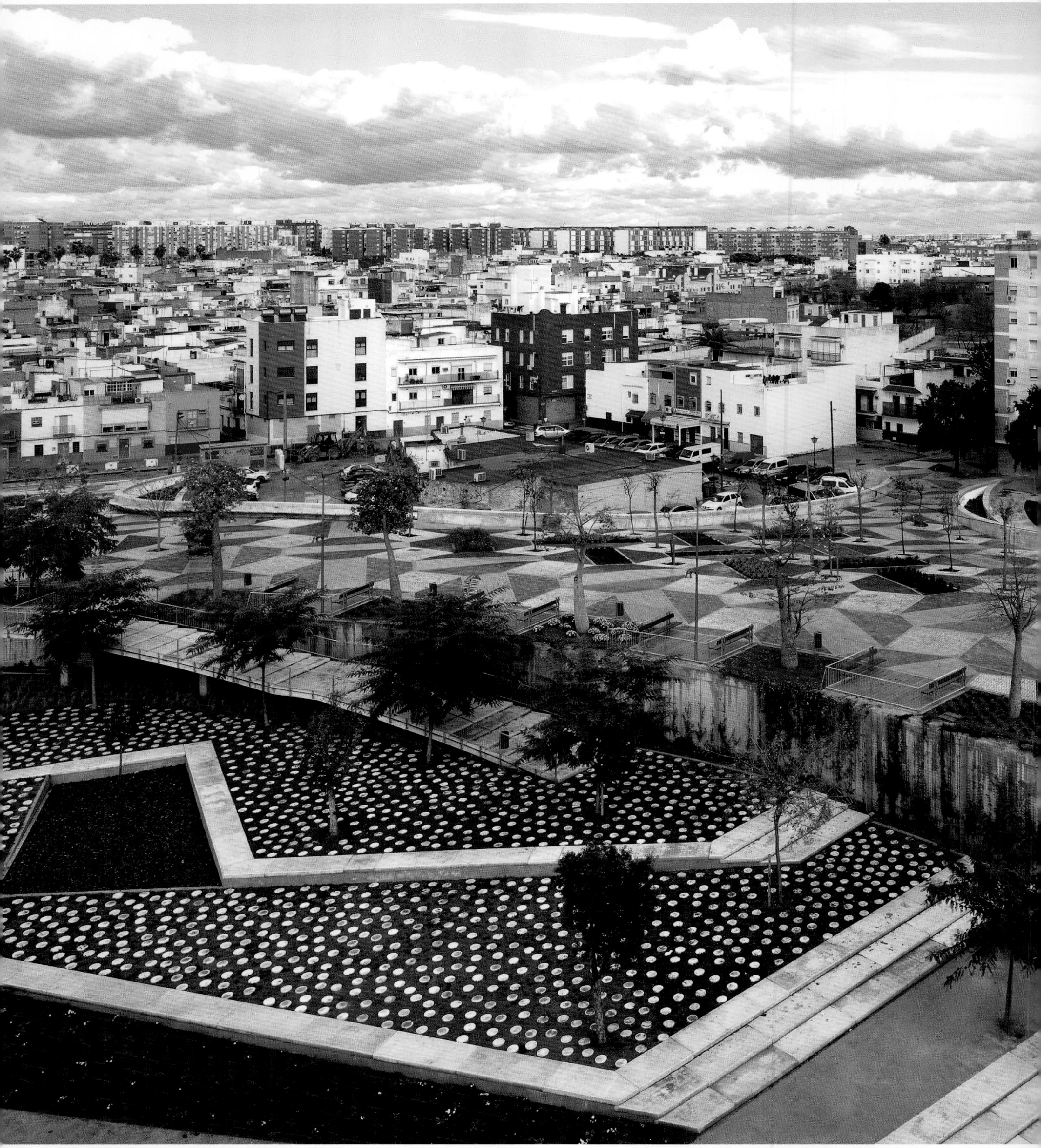

Music Park

Designer: Costa Fierros Arquitectos | **Location:** Sevilla, Spain

The Music Park (Parque de la Música) is located in an existing degraded area, lacking of facilities, and known historically as a land dividing the nearby quarters (Águilas and Los Prunos neighborhoods) and isolating their inhabitants.

The Park is a unique masterplan in terms of urban renovation and integration linked to Sevilla underground infrastructure works. The Park area is 32,487sqm and ensures accessibility to Cocheras Station, located at the center of the Park, and the connectivity between the houses located at both sides of the station.

The new landscape created helps to enjoy a walk around it or having a rest in the designated areas of the Park, and the continuity of the different urban itineraries, making them more convenient and accessible for everybody.

There is a dual purpose: a more cohesive city, regenerated and with better internal connections, and providing a more human and better quality outdoor space and therefore better quality of life for their inhabitants.

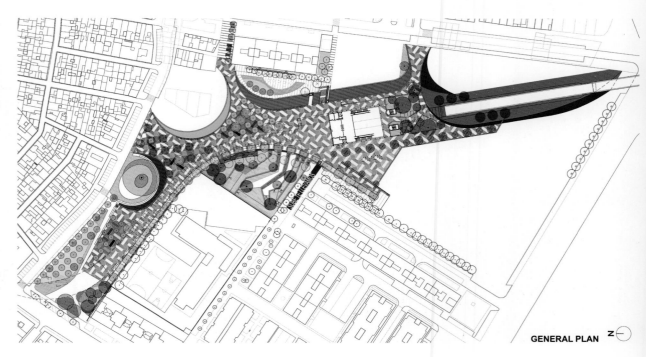

GENERAL PLAN

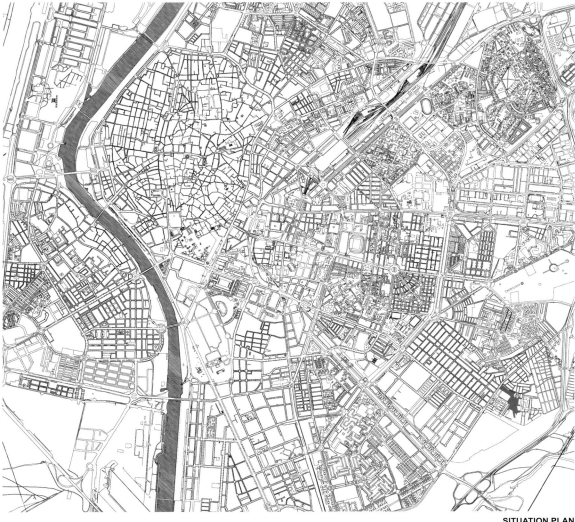

Project name:
Music Park
Completion date:
2011
Principal architects:
Sara Tavares Costa & Pablo F. Díaz-Fierros
Design team:
David Breva, Paula Ferreira, Pedro Rito Nobre, David Ampe, Cristina Rubiño
Quantity:
Antonio Carrascal Cruzado (surveyor)
Structure:
Catsoli S.L.
Installations:
ETINSA
Botanists:
Ernesto Fernández Sanmartín, Sara Tavares Costa
Rendering:
Marcin Sapeta, Alfonso Fiz
Developer:
Agencia de Obra Pública de la Junta de Andalucía
Building contractor:
Rafael Morales S.A., Heliopol, S.A.U.
Site area:
32,487sqm
Budget:
4,544,894.06 Euro
Cost/m^2:
1,400 Euro
Photographer:
Pablo F. Díaz-Fierros

SITUATION PLAN

1. General view
2. Stone bench
3. Singular tree

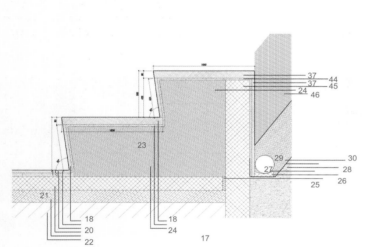
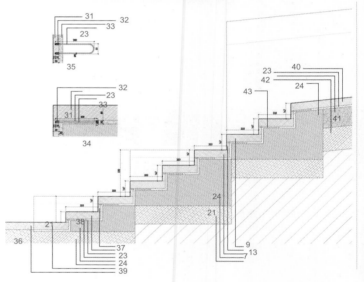

DETAILS

1. Part built in the soil 50mm
   White honed marble. Finished soften
   Special part. Massive pieces of stone
2. White honed marble. Finished soften
3. Belen white granite. Bush hammered finish
4. White honed marble. Finished soften (145 units)
   E=80mm
5. Detail view of section
6. Plan

	X	Y
4 A	1000	950
4B	500	475
4C	1000	1040

7. White honed marble. Finished soften (52 units)
   E=80mm

	X
7A	1000
7B	500

8. White honed marble. Finished soften (18 units)
   Belen white granite. Bush hammered finish (6 units)
   E=80mm

	X
8A	1000
8B	500

9. Belen white granite. Bush hammered finish (3units)
   E=80mm

	W	X	Y	Z
9A	935	1120	930	1235
9B	1010	1000	1000	1120
9C	1150	860	1145	1000

10. Front elevation
    White honed marble. Finished soften (145 units)
    E=30mm

	X	Y
10A	950	425
10B	475	425
10C	950	variable

11. Detail view of section
12. Detail of scale
13. White honed marble. Finished soften (61 units)
    Belen white granite. Bush hammered finish (9 units)
    E=30mm

	X	Y
13A	1000	420
13B	500	420
13C	1000	variable
13D	1150	300
13E	1000	90
13F	500	90

14. Plan of stone bench and circular plaza
15. Section of stone bench and circular plaza
16. Stone bench. Circular plaza
    Elevation view of the circular area
17. Section of stone bench
18. White honed marble 30mm
19. Mortar 40mm
20. 15cm concrete bed. Mesh 8 / 20×20cm
21. Soil compacted to 98% modified proctor 20cm
22. Pre-existing soil
23. Mortar 20mm
24. Perforated brick wall and M-5 mortar
25. Expended polystyrene
26. Mass concrete
27. Draining pipe 200mm
28. Compacted sand
29. Polyeter mesh for revegetation
30. Topsoil
31. Belen white granite or white marble
32. Epoxi resin
33. Stainless steel bar 5
34. Stainless steel bar vertical section
35. Stainless steel bar horizontal section
36. Stone stairs
37. White honed marble 80mm
38. Stainless steel bar 5 and epoxi resin
39. Arypaq type compact paving
40. White bush-hammered Belen granite 80mm
41. Gravel-cement 20cm
42. Soil-subbase 25cm
43. Refer to 35 (stainless steel bar vertical section)
44. Mortar 15mm
45. Reinforced concrete wall
46. Carpet plants: lavender

1. Ceramic pattern
2. Eastern access to the sta
3. Stepped plaza

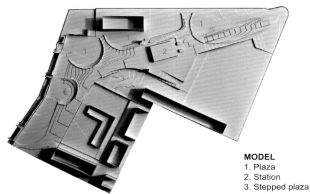

MODEL
1. Plaza
2. Station
3. Stepped plaza

The Park is organized along a north-south promenade that reaches the station level with a gentle slope. Other transversal circulations connect the main promenade with the surrounding streets and plazas.

In the east side, the level difference is solved with retaining walls embracing and protecting the plazas at the surrounding neighborhoods levels. There is an elevator and an escalator next to the station entrance for accessibility.

In the west side, the level difference is resolved with a retaining wall that goes parallel to the underground tunnel and curves itself creating the ramp directing to the main west entrance. There is another elevator for access at the corner between the pedestrian street Águila Marina and Águila de Oro Street.

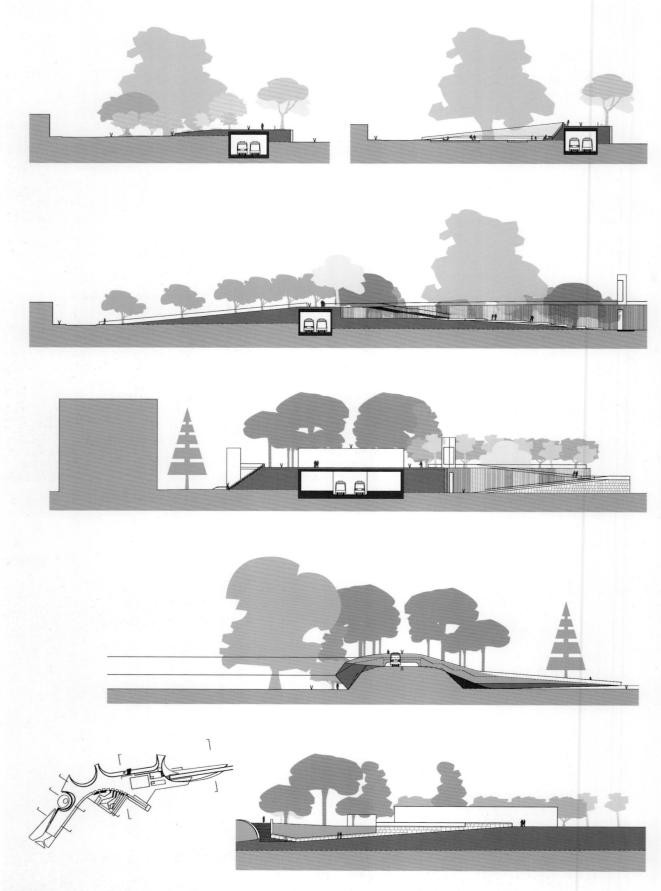

First quality pavement materials have been used: ceramic tiles, lime and granite stones. The patterns are repeated creating a geometry that connects all the different areas in the Park. This pattern is inspired in an existing ceramic pattern in the Patio de Muñecas (Patio of Dolls) from the Reales Alcazares in Sevilla.

1. Wood bench
2. Litter bin, benches and elevator
3. Stairs in stepped plaza
4. Stepped plaza
5. Access ramp

Seventeen flowerbeds in varying sizes are placed in the green landscape. Here a great mix of colorful perennials, flower bulbs and blossoming fruit trees and shrubs are visually inviting people to stay. They enhance and emphasize lush feeling and atmosphere that has become the identity of the garden. The only thing missing is a white rabbit raising its head.

The Hilly Garden is sun exposed during the day and provides various rooms for the visiting citizens. Read a book in the grass, have a picnic with your friends or run with the children up and down the green hills – here there is room for everyone.

The Active Edge marks the transition from the Urban Forest and the quiet street to the Hilly Garden. The edge is an active furniture built in wood.

The 100-meter-long structure that breaks up and down, and shifts between being broad and narrow in the middle of the pocket park, has become a gathering element in the garden. The unprogrammed use of the furniture also stimulates the children's imagination; new games are invented, run, balance, jump, slide, catch.

The Small City Garden of Valby has become a local meeting place, close to the streets and the city life. Here you will find a small green break in a busy weekday and the weekend destination for the local citizens. The various green elements in the garden emphasize the ever-changing expression of nature over the years: spring, summer, autumn and winter…

1. Children playing around the Active Edge
2-3. The Small City Garden offers a meeting place for local residents

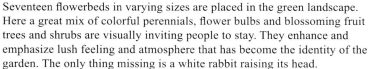

UC Davis West Village

Designer: SWA | **Location:** Davis, California, USA

UC Davis West Village is a new campus neighborhood located on UC Davis land adjacent to the core campus in Davis, California. The dynamic mixed-use community is designed to enable faculty, staff and students to live near campus, take advantage of environmentally friendly transportation options, and participate fully in campus life.

The West Village Master Plan was a response to the substantive growth in the number of students, faculty and staff on the Davis campus. Rapidly escalating housing costs have forced campus affiliates to seek housing outside of Davis. The West Village residences and apartments provide new choices for those who desire to live, work, and recreate in a sustainable residential neighborhood that is seamlessly integrated with UC Davis' core activities.

Project name:
UC Davis West Village
Completion date:
2011
Mixed-Use Architects:
Studio E Architects
Residential Architects:
Lim Chang Rohling & Associates
Civil Engineering:
Cunningham Engineering
Client:
Carmel Partners
Site area:
81ha
Project area:
52.6ha
Building area:
4,180sqm
Programs:
Retail, 343 faculty staff homes,
2,000 student beds
Photographer:
Jonnu Singleton
Awards:
2013 ULI Global Excellence Award

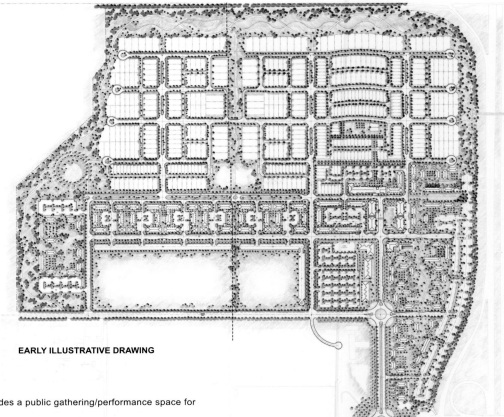

EARLY ILLUSTRATIVE DRAWING

1. The amphitheater stage at the Village Square provides a public gathering/performance space for local festivals/special events
2. Outdoor amenities at the West Village Center include recreational swimming and lap pools, sand volleyball courts and an outdoor kitchen/barbecue area for parties/special events

ARTIST'S RENDERING OF THE RAMBLE STUDENT APARTMENTS

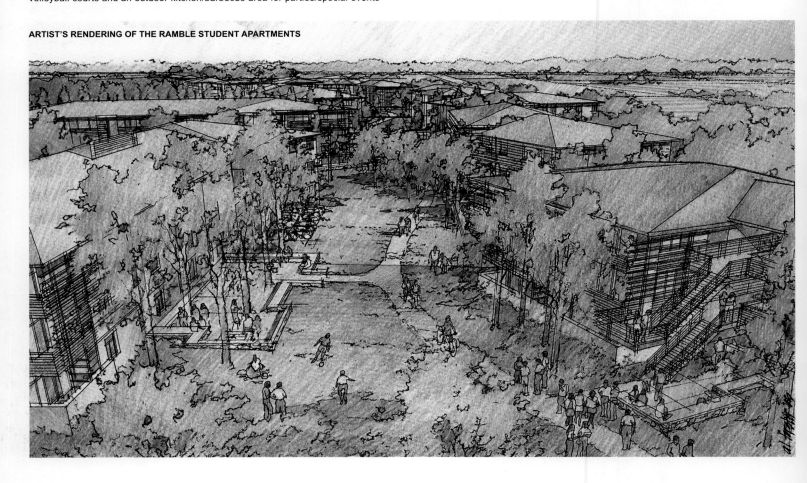

The implementation plan is based on three core principles: housing affordability, environmental responsiveness, and quality of place.

• Housing Availability. New housing options will enable faculty and staff to purchase new homes locally, at below market prices, and will expand the choices for students to live near campus.

• Environmental Responsiveness. Sustainable design of the site and the buildings will reduce reliance on cars, limit energy consumption, enable energy production, and contribute to a healthy environment.

• Quality of Place. A network of open spaces, parks, gardens, pathways and courtyards will provide the attributes and character of traditional Davis neighborhoods. The project is the largest zero net energy development of its kind in the U.S. Employing revolutionary energy efficiency measures and meeting the community's energy demands through on-site solar power generation, West Village introduces a new model for environmentally responsible living.

Advanced energy conservation measures, use of energy-efficient appliances and optimized solar orientation in the site design has resulted in a reduced energy load that exceeds building standards by more than 50%. Achieving the goal of zero net energy is accomplished by reducing the community energy demand through energy-efficient building measures while producing an on-site renewable energy supply. Other sustainable measure included integrating storm drainage and five miles (approx. 8km) of bicycle-pedestrian paths into an extensive open space system of parks, greenways, ponds, gardens, and sports facilities.

In addition to 343 homes for faculty and staff, the plan provides approximately one thousand student apartments organized around informal, interconnected courtyards. The community focuses on a mixed-use Village Center with retail and civic space, 94 residential apartments, and a Village Green. It also includes elementary, high school and community college facilities. Continuous cross-campus bicycle routes allow for easy transportation and circulation around the campus, creating a new sustainable residential community for UC Davis students.

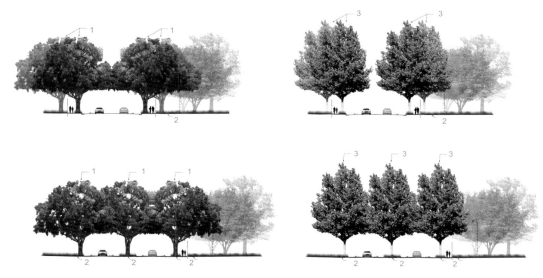

ENTRY LANDSCAPE SECTIONS – OPTION 1 ALTERNATIVES
1. Cork oak
2. Drainage ditch
3. London plane tree

Option 1 with Quercus suber

Option 1 with Platanus acerifolia 'Bloodgood'

1-3. The West Village offers a variety of public spaces; from active courtyards adjacent to student housing encouraging community/outdoor living to passive stormwater retention/detention gardens integrated throughout the project
4. Connectivity to the University's Core Campus is easy at the West Village with its system of multi-use bike/pedestrian trails
5. Rushes, grasses and sedges adjacent to the Village Square intercept stormwater runoff and provide treatment before water is piped offsite

Lemvig Skatepark

Designer: EFFEKT
Location: Lemvig, Denmark

1. Lemvig Skatepark is situated in beautiful surroundings on an old industrial site on the harbor
2. The concept – to merge the traditional skatepark with a typical recreational park

"By introducing the 'Skate+Park' concept, EFFEKT has created a new type of multi-functional and recreational urban park area that bridges user groups of diverse interests and age."

1. The Skatepark features a variety of recreational functions
2. A street basketball area, a picnic area with barbeques and a playground for the youngest children
3. Skateboard competition in the big bowl
4. A skateboarder grinds a rail in front of the outdoor fitness area

In the spring of 2013, Lemvig Municipality faced a group of citizens eager to transform an empty industrial lot on the city's harbor front into an area of leisure and recreation. In order to meet the demands of the local population, EFFEKT worked closely with representatives from different user groups to develop a new type of urban space. The result of this collaboration was an integrated skatepark + urban park that offered a range of programmatic features and recreational opportunities. Set in beautiful surroundings, the park has created a new social space in Lemvig, attracting skaters and families from the entire region.

"The harbor, having displaced most of its activity along the coast, had become a residual waterscape of maritime activity. By envisioning the Skate+Park as a social gathering space that would attract people of all ages and interests, we believed it could become a catalyst for revitalization that would re-brand the harbor front as a recreational hub and re-introduce the harbor as an important asset to the city," says Mikkel Bøgh of EFFEKT.

"From the start, we knew that the project would need an array of ingredients to differentiate itself from the gray, black and rust-tinted surfaces of the immediate surroundings – the consequence of a downturn in the local fishing industry. By challenging the typology of the skatepark – an otherwise mono-

PLAN

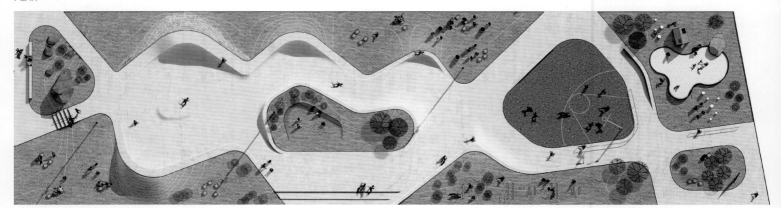

3

Project name:
Lemvig Skatepark
Completion date:
2013
Lead designers:
Sinus Lynge & Tue Hesselberg
Foged
Consultant:
Glifberg + Lykke
Client:
Lemvig Municipality, Realdania,
Lokale og Anlægsfonden
General contractor:
Søren V. Jensen
Skatepark contractor:
Beaver Concrete
Site area:
2,200sqm
Photographer:
EFFEKT & Mads Krabbe

4

functional grayscape – alongside a thorough investigation on the dichotomy of surface in public space, we were able to design a hybrid platform that would accommodate a multitude of social and recreational activities. Skateboarding originated in streets, co-existing with a multitude of other urban activities. As it grew in popularity and commercialized, the sport and culture was moved into these gray parks where it became isolated from the same city that originally fuelled, challenged and inspired the skaters. By merging skateboarding with a multitude of other recreational activities and re-introducing the (skate) culture back into the heart city center, we feel that both skateboarders and other groups of the population will benefit greatly from this new co-existence on the harbor, and potentially breathe new life into an otherwise abandoned area with great potentials."

Lemvig Skatepark is part of the public space program "Byg-Det-Op" (Build It!) orchestrated by Danish Architecture Center and Danish Broadcasting Corporation in collaboration with Realdania, the Danish Foundation for Culture and Sport Facilities, Danish Arts Foundation and COWI. The project was conducted as a Design-Build project in a period of four months in the summer of 2013. The entire project was documented by Danish television in four individual documentaries.

DETAILS

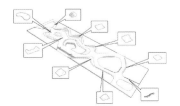

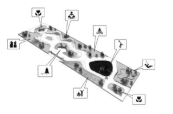

1. Top view of the shade
2. The park is structured following the traces of the old houses

Remodeling Work on Riera de La Salut

Designer: Pol Femenias Arquitectes (PFA)

Location: Sant Feliu de Llobregat, Barcelona, Spain

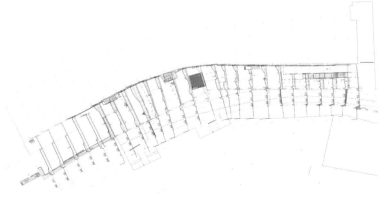

DIFFERENT SECTIONS: EACH SLICE HAS ITS OWN TOPOGRAPHY

The intervention takes place in the middle of one of the densest neighborhoods in Sant Feliu de Llobregat, near Barcelona. A working-class neighborhood, grown around the old textile factories, wall to wall, with humble dwellings of the workers themselves. The demolition of one of the last factories still standing was used to build underground parking to supply the district of La Salut, leaving the place where the factory was a large gap in the form of concrete cover for this parking.

The proposal extended the existing walls of the old houses, shaping each parterre of the park. As slices of bread, the public space is composed by different corners of smaller scale, almost domestic, with the will to make visitors feel comfortable in a more accessible area by fragmenting it. Thus, each section is designed uniquely in both plan and section, creating topographies that shelter and insulate the walker from the adjacent road.

The emptiness left by the old factory exposed the walls of the old houses, previously hidden, which now became the facade of the public space. The choice of ceramics as a material to cover those old walls was almost automatic. The ceramics cooked at high temperature allowed the architects to work with an inexpensive, strong material, guaranteeing an optimal aging in front of frost, rain and temperature changes.

Project name:
Remodeling Work on Riera de La Salu
Completion date:
2013
Architect:
Pol Femenias
Client:
Sant Feliu de Llobregat City Hall
Site area:
approx. 5,000sqm
Photographer:
O.M Estudi
Awards:
2014 The 12th ASCER Tile of Spain
Awards, First Prize in the Architecture
Category

1. Pathway along the lattice wall
2. Topographies create dunes that keep
pedestrians away from the road

It was the architects' intention to recover the ceramic industrial past as a memory of the site and, at the same time, as a replica of the walls of the existing patios. The new wall would incorporate the richness of the old walls, a collage of textures and holes, reflecting different states and interventions that the city had suffered over time. Only a wall composed by ceramic pieces allowed the architects to sift the vision of those backyards, and yet incorporate its irregularities, twists and exceptions.

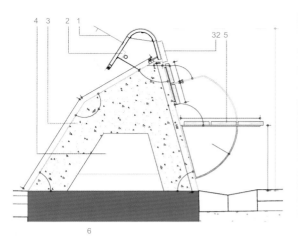

CONTINOUS BENCH SEPARATING THE PARK FROM THE ROAD

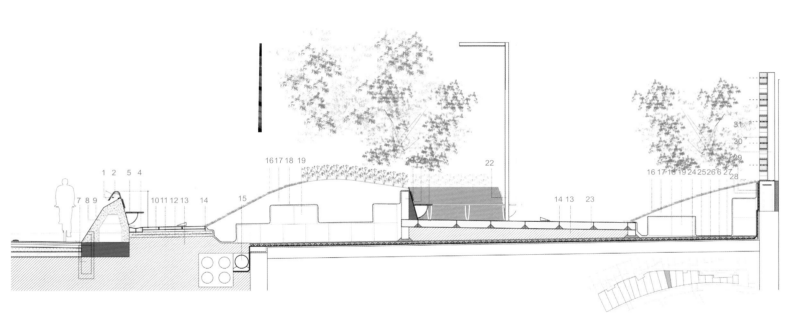

CROSS SECTION OF A PIECE OF TOPOGRAPHY

SECTIONS

1. Registration Corten steel plate with clip closure and concealed screws
2. Luminaire ROURA fluorescence -1000 ESU LED integrated element
3. Median reinforced concrete with shuttering to go lined with separator element according to lighting model Roura
4. Prefabricated concrete canal Breinco
5. Bank pine on supports c/100cm matte stainless steel. Color to choose by DF
6. Anti-root band
7. Prefabricated drainage pipe with vertical Corten steel grid
8. Median reinforced concrete with shuttering to go lined with separator element according to lighting model Roura
9. ESU-1000 separator element of Formtube
10. Precast concrete slab Breinco Vulcano, 60×40×8cm; ash (70%), sand (30%)
11. Mixing mortar layer
12. Base reinforced concrete floor 15/P/20 HM
13. Land compacted 98% P.M.
14. Corten steel deck 20cm; e: 10mm; anchor c/50mm
15. Drainage tube

16. Geotextile protector
17. Zincoterra topsoil
18. Geotextile layer
19. Styrofoam blocks, d = 10, 60×60×50cm, mounted latch and sealed with polyurethane foam
20. Compacted concrete wall
21. Corten steel plate coat
22. Luminaire ROURA fluorescence
23. Stone plate, 20×60cm
24. Filtering system
25. Lime with sands
26. ISM50 fixation and protecting mat
27. Anti-root waterproofing layer
28. Waterproofing rubber sheet, with a minimum of 30cm above waterproofing layer
29. Concrete parapet wall, with an average height of 1.20m
30. Tubular column 180×180 fixed to wall; ceramic truss bracing; all galvanized in workshop
31. SF ceramic lattice of Cumella, supported at each 4.5m, formed by three types of woods, colors to decide according to DF
32. Components, glazed or matte according to DF

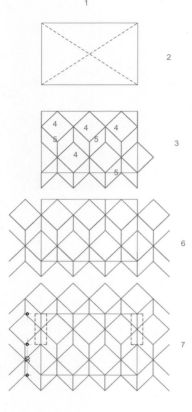

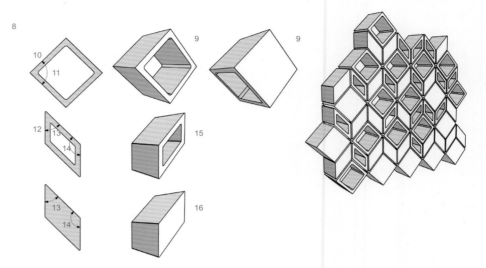

By determining a simple geometry, with the fewest parts possible, the architects got sufficient resources to cover a facade of 150m and incorporate the requirements of the existing enclosures. First, the wall should keep the coronation of the existing walls, made of different materials and with different heights, tracing as well as possible a continuous horizon that wrapped them all. Second, the architects needed to maintain the varying degrees of opacity that those walls had, going from block walls to fully transparent fences. The ceramic wall should allow them to incorporate these different gradations and textures, and should do it in a continuous finish throughout the park.

WALL PRODUCTION
1. Construction scheme
2. Main module: 89×60
3. Pieces layout:
   1 module = 6 pieces type 4
            = 12 pieces type 5
6. Horizontal reinforcement:
   Folded murfor 150 galvanized armor every two rows
7. Vertical reinforcement:
   180×180mm galvanized steel columns anchored to concrete wall every 4.45m, with horizontal bars fixed into ceramics every two rows. Everything galvanized.
8. Geometry
9. Ceramic cube cooked at high temperatures 20×20×20cm, walls 20mm width, according to CERAMIC CUMELLA. Placed front or across according to plants. Colors determined by architect.
10. 200mm
11. 90°
12. 134mm
13. 45°
14. 135°
15. Ceramic extruded rombe cooked at high temperature, 20×20×12.4cm, walls 20mm width, according to CERAMIC CUMELLA. Colors determined by architect.
16. Ceramic extruded rombe hollowed cooked at high temperature, 20×20×12.4cm, walls 20mm width, according to CERAMIC CUMELLA. Colors determined by architect.
17. COLORS
   The chromatic palette for the ceramics came from the tones of the exiting facades. By limiting the image to seven colors, along with the ceramics color itself, the architects had the eight colors for the latticework. These eight tones, with a glossy or matte finishing, applied to whether opaque or transparent ceramics,

allowed the architects to include in the latticework all the subtleties they were seeking for.
18. Color 00 (color base ceramics)
19. Color 01
   R=255
   G=255
   B= 255
20. Color 02
   R=215
   G=242
   B= 225
21. Color 03
   R=206
   G=204
   B= 191
22. Color 04
   R=237
   G=209
   B= 170
23. Color 05
   R=203
   G=163
   B= 111
24. Color 06
   R=185
   G=170
   B= 135
25. Color 07
   R=127
   G=92
   B= 72

1. Bench & Bus Shelter Design by Urban Movement, New Youk
2. Bus stop
3. Aerial view of athlete village

Whistler Olympic Village, Cheakamus Crossing

Designer: Tom Barratt Ltd.

Location: Whistler, British Columbia, Canada

Located in the Canadian ski resort of Whistler, the Whistler Olympic Village was home to more than 3,000 Olympic and Paralympic athletes during the 2010 Olympic and Paralympic Winter Games.

Following the Games, more than 800 local residents will call the Village home in the new neighborhood called Cheakamus Crossing. This new, green neighborhood is one of the legacies of the 2010 Winter Games. It includes multi-use space for the Whistler Gymnastics Club and the Whistler Adaptive Sports Program.

Contained within Cheakamus Crossing is the Whistler Athletes Center. With its lodge and townhome accommodation, and High Performance Center it is the epicenter of athlete training and development in Whistler.

The design of the Olympic Village had to incorporate all the requirements of an Olympic Village for the games period and be rapidly converted for resident use.

The Village is pedestrian oriented with a central open space community meeting area adjacent to an International Youth Hostel and restaurant. Patios and children's play area encourage residents to meet.

The Village is adjacent to and established network of walking, hiking and mountain biking trails. It also backs onto the wilderness of river, lakes and mountains.

The design of the central commons meeting area is formal at the edges breaking into an informal natural edge along the children's play area and the patio edge follows the flow pattern of the nearby Cheakamus River.

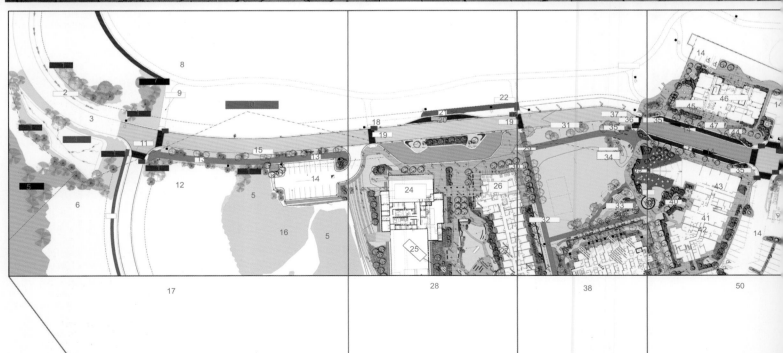

1. Walking trails and stone bench

Project name:
Whistler Olympic Village,
Cheakamus Crossing
Site area:
18.7ha
Photographer:
Robin O'Neill

The Village blends with
the natural surroundings in
architectural style and by an
ecological landscape design
utilizing native planting.

Research and reference was
made to the surrounding forest
and vegetation to help guide the
choice of planting, colors and
rock used in the site.

courtyard plaza
29. Athlete gateway
30. Outdoor patio
31. Tree pockets line street frame views from
Commons
32. Low landscape concrete walls frame
edges of Commons
33. Children play discover landscape
34. Overlook Berm
35. Natural planted areas at corners bulge
36. Brushed concrete crosswalk
37. Transition to main street unit paving &
street trees
38. Commons park (open lawn public space
gateway legacy feature kids play, patios,
seating)
39. Raised patio
40. Planting buffer & concrete wall
41. Lot 8
42. Residential
43. Commercial
44. Street trees in tree grate
45. Restaurant patio seating sunny spot with
low planting buffer to sidewalk
46. Whistler Hostel
47. Sidewalk unit paving
48. Tree lined and landscaped along parking
entry road
49. Lot 10
Proposed live / work
50. Urban street
A more formal streetscape design
51. Valley trail
52. 2m wide sidewalk
53. 1.5m wide sidewalk
54. Native forest planting theme
55. Rehabilitation
Native planting / revegetation along valley
trail & sidewalk
56. Entry signature
57. Existing gravel trail
58. Entry feature / village signature
59. Retain existing forest slope as backdrop
to entry feature
60. Entry through natural forest
Existing forest along entry road
Feature rain garden catchment

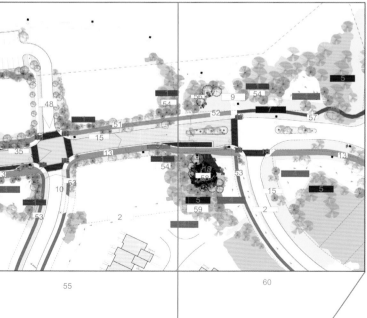

STREETSCAPE PLAN
1. Rehabilitation enhancement
2. Rain garden feature native / filtration
planting
3. Road continues
4. Detention pond filtration planting
5. Existing native forest
6. Lot 1
7. Connection to existing trail systems
8. Park lighting & design to be determined
9. Proposed pedestrian access to future park
10. Future park
11. Brushed concrete crosswalks
12. Lot 5
13. 3m wide asphalt
14. Parking
15. Native plant pockets highlight boulevard
16. Retain existing forested knoll
17. Rehabilitation natural forest & knoll rain
gardens trail access
18. Curb cut
19. Brushed concrete crosswalks
20. Bus stop
21. Brushed concrete
22. Park lighting & design to be determined
23. Lodge-services & drop-off lay by
24. High Performance Center
25. Hydro kloak
- 0.8m drainrock surround
- gravel pathway, 2 stairs access
- concrete pad elevation 613.3
- planting screening around
26. Athlete lodge
27. Landscape plant bed shade trees
28. Athlete center entry drop-off / bus stop

An innovative stormwater management system was developed by Ker Wood Leidal Consulting Engineers for the entire site drainage. The landscape design around the buildings and along the roadsides integrates comprehensive rain gardens into the system.

A heat exchanger has been incorporated into the waste water treatment plant, removing heat from the effluent and distributing temperate water throughout the site to each of the homes.

An adjacent landfill has been decommissioned and capped and served as a warehouse site during the Games and then become a park. The Village has become a thriving local community providing much needed affordable housing in Whistler.

Visible Social Neighborhood Activity

Although the size of retail/ commercial uses is not large, they are placed to create a central critical mass of visible activity. The sitting places on the edge of the Commons would be visible from the road and from the deli/market. The knoll and the related terrace, south of building A, would also be visible and would invite people to move onward into the natural landscape.

The Village Crossroads

The open spaces corridor extending from the Cheakamus River and the regional trail system to the community recreation fields is one arm of the crossroads. The other is the road and trail system crossing through the village core which invariably is the place of greatest social activity; this is the place where the diverse population meets for daily activities and special events. The Commons is the centerpiece of the crossroads.

The concept of the Cheakamus Area Legacy Neighborhood is derived from connecting the power of the social landscape and the enduring Olympic program, with a set of sustainable neighborhood design principles.

The Cheakamus River is the most prominent natural feature in the area, and embodies the natural energy of this site. The river and other landscape characteristics provide the armature for this neighborhood, giving it a structure that inspires the design individually and cannot be replicated elsewhere. Around this armature, an Olympic program will be built, providing an enduring legacy of facilities that serve the whole municipally, and memories of the Games for generations to come.

ATHLETE VILLAGE LANDSCAPE
1. Future park & trails post Olympic
2. Commons park
3. Natural forest & rock knoll retained
4. Knoll retained
5. Detention pond

1. The green area and the entrance
2. View of the stone trails along Cheakamus River

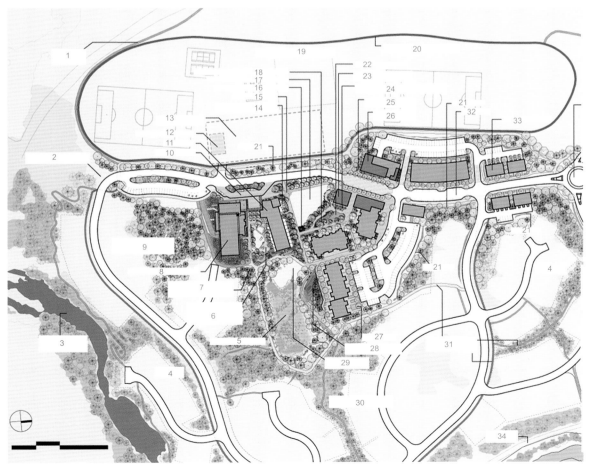

ATHLETE VILLAGE EARLY SITE PLANNING
1. To the dump connection to "Sea to Sky Trail"
2. Visual terminus of main street public art opportunity
3. Natural basalt rock formation – eeological historical feature
4. Residential development
5. Wetland
6. "Small Commons" shared hard and soft flex space spill out space from gym, dance rooms and hotel
7. Natural landscape transition small knoll & screening at the back of Athlete Center
8. Whistler High Performance Center
9. This knoll is an important landscape form. It should be preserved as a public park.
10. Vehicular drop-off
11. Athlete Lodge
12. Potential site for fieldhouse
13. Possible children's play and park activities
14. Glared restaurant & seasonal outdoor dining patio
15. Gateway icon feature
16. Public gathering-file pit & seating
17. The "Commons" public outdoor space
18. Feature landscape rain garden
19. Landfill used as transportation center during Olympics / future park
20. Running/training multi-purpose loop around play fields
21. Rain gardens
22. Space for kids play
23. Retail commercial primarily used as pub & restaurant
24. Terrace for tables, chairs, benches with views of Commons, kids play & rain garden feature
25. Outdoor market terrace tables and chairs
26. Retail / commercial possible market / dell
27. Private gardens
28. Preserved knoll, a remain of the natural landscape
29. Terraced grass slope sunny view spot
30. The green spine ephemeral stream corridor
31. Pedestrian passageways internal neighborhood sidewalk and train links
32. Main street
33. Live/work townhouses
34. Westside main logging road
35. Feature / remain of entrance to Olympics athlete village public art opportunity

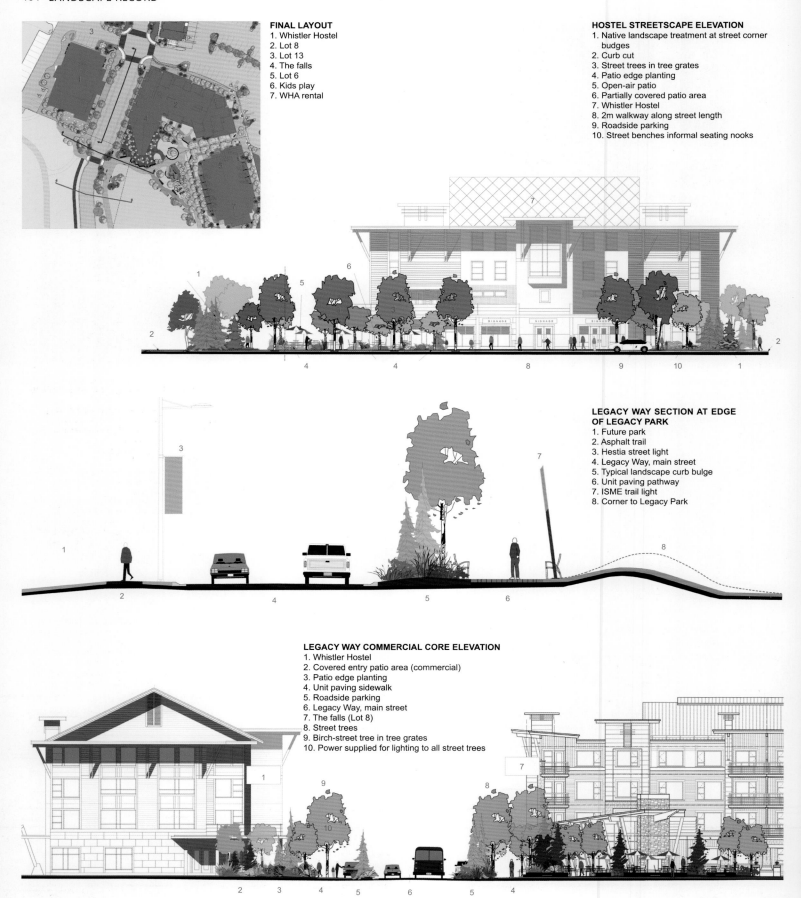

FINAL LAYOUT
1. Whistler Hostel
2. Lot 8
3. Lot 13
4. The falls
5. Lot 6
6. Kids play
7. WHA rental

HOSTEL STREETSCAPE ELEVATION
1. Native landscape treatment at street corner budges
2. Curb cut
3. Street trees in tree grates
4. Patio edge planting
5. Open-air patio
6. Partially covered patio area
7. Whistler Hostel
8. 2m walkway along street length
9. Roadside parking
10. Street benches informal seating nooks

LEGACY WAY SECTION AT EDGE OF LEGACY PARK
1. Future park
2. Asphalt trail
3. Hestia street light
4. Legacy Way, main street
5. Typical landscape curb bulge
6. Unit paving pathway
7. ISME trail light
8. Corner to Legacy Park

LEGACY WAY COMMERCIAL CORE ELEVATION
1. Whistler Hostel
2. Covered entry patio area (commercial)
3. Patio edge planting
4. Unit paving sidewalk
5. Roadside parking
6. Legacy Way, main street
7. The falls (Lot 8)
8. Street trees
9. Birch-street tree in tree grates
10. Power supplied for lighting to all street trees

FINAL LAYOUT
1. Park
2. Legacy Way
3. Legacy Park
4. Athlete Lodge
5. High Performance Center
6. Lot 5

**LEGACY WAY TERMINUS MEDIAN
TYPICAL STREETSCAPE SECTION**
1. Retained knoll featuring existing vegetation
2. ISMA trail light
3. Sidewalk 1.5m
4. Hestia street light (with banner)
5. Legacy Way road
6. Landscape terminus median
7. Hestia street light (with street sign & hanging basket)
8. Edge of capped landfill future park design

**HIGH PERFORMANCE CENTER STREETSCAPE
SECTION**
1. Low concrete planter for snow shed and seating
2. "Shad grove" of birch trees in the tree grates
3. Covered walkway between High Performance Center and Athlete Lodge
4. Athlete Center & Lodge drop-off
5. Landscape median
6. Legacy Way, main street
7. Future park / play fields

1. Installation of low-energy LED bike trail lights
2. Playground and sport facilities
3. Bike Rack Stretching Bar by Urban Movement, New York

Athelete Village Plants	
BOTANICAL NAME	COMMON NAME
Trees	
Amelanchier x grandiflora 'Princess Diana'	Princess Diana Serviceberry
Betula papyrifera (Triple/Single Stems)	Paper Birch
Chamaecyparis nootkatensis	Yellow Cedar
Picea glauca	White Spruce
Pinus uncinata	Mountain Pine
Populus tremuloides	Trembling Aspen
Tsuga mertensiana	Mountain Hemlock
Shrubs	
Acer glabrum	Douglas Maple
Amelanchier alnifolia	Serviceberry
Azalea 'Pink Lights'	Azalea
Azalea 'White Lights'	Azalea
Cornus stolonifera	Redtwig Dogwood
Pinus mugo pumilio	Mugo Pine
Rosa Baffin	Baffin Rose
Rosa explorer 'Frontenac'	Frontenac Rose (deep pink)
Rosa explorer 'Simon Fraser'	Simon Fraser Rose (med pink)
Rosa rugosa 'Jens Munk'	Jens Munk Rugosa Rose (med pink)
Rosa woodsii	Wood's Rose
Rhododendron PJM	Rhododendron
Rhododendron ramapo	Rhododendron
Rubus parviflorus	Thimbleberry
Vaccinium parviflorum	Red Huckleberry
Ornamental Grasses	
Alopecurus pratensis Aureovariegatus	Golden foxtail
Arrhenatherum bulbosum	Bulbous oat grass
Calamagrostis x acutifolia 'Karl Foerster'	Feather Reed Grass
Carex grayi	Gray's sedge
Deschampsia caespitosa 'Bronzeschleier'	Bronzeschlieier Tufted Hair Grass
Deschampsia caespitosa 'Fairy's Joke'	Fairy's Joke Tufted Hair Grass
Koeleria macrantha	June Grass
Elymus cinerus	Wild Rye
Festuca glauca	Blue fescue
Juncus effusus 'Spiralis'	Lesser corkscrew rush
Helictotrichon sempervirens	Blue Oat Grass
Miscanthus floridulus	Morning light maiden grass
Miscanthus floridulus	Giant Miscanthus
Miscanthus sinensis purpurascens	Flame Grass
Pennisetum alopecuroides	Fountain Grass

Features & Sustainability

- Installation of low-energy LED bike trail lights; first use in North America
- Focus on accessibility in all areas for Paralympic games
- A stormwater management system and wetland complex created on site for stormwater retention, treatment and habitat enhancement

Rain-Gardens: Drainage & Sustainablity

The tiny scream channel passing along edges of streets and Commons is to convey the sense that natural systems move through the village core, implying a connection from the mountain tops to the river.

The Senses

Buildings are placed so that the major public places have morning sunlight and optimum views to the northwest.

Athelete Village Plants	
BOTANICAL NAME	**COMMON NAME**
Ferns	
Blechnum spicant	Deer Fern
Polystichum munitum	Sword Fern
Groundcovers	
Arctostaphyllos uva-ursi	Kinnickinnick
Perennials	
Aquilegia formosa	Red Columbine
Camassia quamash	Common camas
Coreopsis verticillata 'Moonbeam'	Moonbeam Tickseed
Hosta 'Patriot'	Patriot Hosta
Iberis sempervirens 'snowflake'	Candytuft
Ligularia stenocephala 'The Rocket'	Rocket
Lonicera 'Dropmore Scarlet'	Climbing Honeysuckle
Nepeta x 'Dropmore Blue'	Dropmore Blue Catmint
Penstemon fruticosus 'Purple Haze'	Beard-Tongue
Rudbeckia fulgida 'Goldsturm'	Goldsturm Cone Flower
Rudbeckia nitida 'herbstonne'	Herbstonne Rudbeckia

1. Detail of grass in the green field

COMMONS WALLS
1. Conc. W / smooth finish reinf. as required, color as specified
2. Finish grade (slope away)
3. Planting soil mix as specified
4. Prepared subgrade
5. Conc. footing reinf. as required
6. 100mm drain pipe placed entire length of wall
7. Aggregate backfill
8. 40mm weeps 3m O.C.

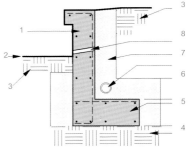

COMMONS SECTION
1. Open lawn
2. Pathway through Commons
3. Rain garden
4. Stone bench set in grass berm
5. Small trickle of recirculating water - kids play / discovery
6. Sand, logs, rocks natural play area
7. Small grass berm & aspen grove
8. Walkway
9. Stone seating wall / retaining raised lawn
10. Grass slope up / to shady rest area
11. Lawn & planting
12. Restaurant patio
13. Building / restaurant

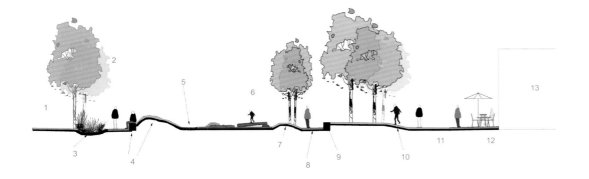

ATHLETE VILLAGE HOUSING BUILDING B2
ROOF RUN-OFF DRAINAGE
1. Commons unit paver pathway
2. Weep holes
3. 2%
4. Planting & seating edge along Commons wall
5. Berm
6. Wall
7. Sit wall
8. Planting
9. Topsoil
10. Topsoil
11. 60 mil polyethylene liner
12. 25mm minus (Typ) round river rock
13. Perforated pipe
14. Filter cloth
15. Treatment soil & root zone:
    Engineered soil
    40% sand
    25% topsoil
    35% compost-wood chips
16. Subgrade
17. 50mm minus gravel
18. 19mm minus crushed gravel
19. 25-40mm bedding sand
20. Old country stone pavers w / sand filled cracks

21. Concrete block
22. Building
23. Semi-enclosed patio
24. Roof drip line
25. Centerline of rain garden
26. Mixed native plants
27. Ponding depth-0.2m
28. Galvanized steel grate over rain garden

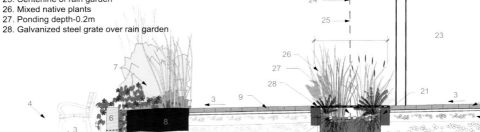

Irwell City Park

Designer: FoRM Associates

Irwell City Park is a vision of a river and its corridor, which has been reclaimed by its surrounding communities; of a river transformed from a barrier into a meeting place; of a river moved from the periphery to the very heart of the cities' shared life and identity. The projected scope of change along the Irwell corridor over the next decade is huge and the three partner authorities recognize the vital importance to once again provide the unifying thread that links the multitude of disparate developments already built and anticipated along its banks.

The concept of the new linear park overcomes the effects of previous industrialization by transforming the river corridor from a major polluted severance into a premier public realm with Irwell River at its heart. Irwell Park will transform the currently neglected river corridor into a powerful symbol of connectivity, synergy and unity for Greater Manchester. Its impact will be momentous for the North West region, delivering significant economic gains at a time when the economic climate is under stress, creating a solid foundation for future private and public sector investment.

Project name:
Irwell City Park
Client:
Manchester City Council,
Salford RUC and Trafford
Metropolitan Authority
Awards:
Highly Commended in
category Urban Design and
Masterplanning, Landscape
Institute Awards 2008

ACTIVITY CONCEPT

Location: Manchester, UK

Photographer: FoRM Associates

Area: 0.25 acres

The masterplan comprises of a continuous alphabet of pedestrian and cycling routes along the river, several major squares, three new pedestrian bridges, regeneration of heritage sites, ecological preservation of the river, new pocket parks and regeneration of large green areas in North Manchester.

This new park, on a scale of urbanism rarely seen in the UK, will become the jewel in the crown of the new Manchester: Knowledge Capital, celebrating its unique heritage and creating one of the most vibrant, exciting and desirable waterfront destinations in Europe.

Some featured sections of Irwell Park include:

Cathedral Square

The redesign of the Cathedral Square creates a premier public realm setting for the Manchester Cathedral. The new square will deliver a fully pedestrianized space re-establishing the connection between the river Irwell and the Cathedral. The planned relocation of the vehicular traffic from the front of cathedral onto the opposite river bank will not only address the current condition of acute severance but will also create a new gateway space linking central Manchester and Salford new Greengate Quarter. The re-establishing of the connection to the river Irwell will help to open the economic regeneration of the Cathedral arches into a prime restaurant/visitor attraction usage.

Cathedral Walk

One of the most ambitious and dramatic features of Irwell City Park will be a 250m, snaking footbridge. The Cathedral Walk will provide a spectacular route over the water, through the deep urban canyon formed by high buildings along both banks. The walkway will recreate the historical views of the Cathedral along the river turning the Cathedral into a genuine focal point of the route. The proposal is a pragmatic means of overcoming the sense of separation between the river and the city at this juncture and of achieving continuous access along the river itself.

Albert Gardens

Albert Gardens integrates a previously fragmented and dysfunctional public realm into a new cohesive riverfront. The new design provides a narrative of badly needed breakout spaces within the newly built high density office, hotel and residential developments.

CONCEPT
1. The meadows green bowl recreation
2. Broughton urban green
3. Transition node green gateway
4. Canyon
5. Hot spot civic
6. Greengate
7. Magic river
8. Urban river
9. Heritage industry interpretation
10. Chapel wharf
11. Castlefield
12. Ordsall urban blue
13. Pomona
14. Transition node ecology gateway
15. Salford quays blue bowl media arts sport

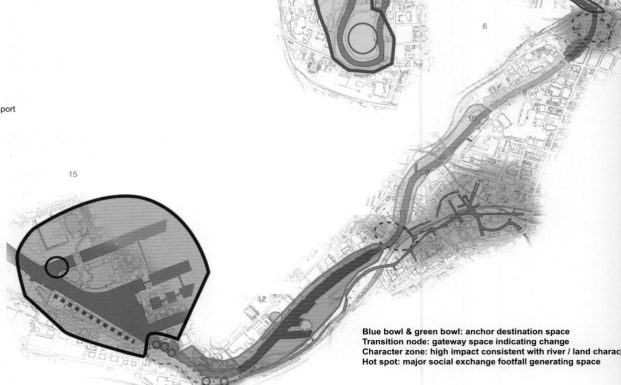

Blue bowl & green bowl: anchor destination space
Transition node: gateway space indicating change
Character zone: high impact consistent with river / land charac
Hot spot: major social exchange footfall generating space

Clippers Quay

Focused around the vast expense of water at its center, the southern end of the park will become a vibrant, dynamic hub of activity. The new development of Media City UK as one of the region's major economic drivers, along with success of The Lowry and Imperial War Museum North, will draw people along the new routes created by Irwell City Park both for business and pleasure.

photos © Stefania Facco

In the Allmende-Kontor community garden, people from different cultural backgrounds grow plants and food

Un–gated Community Gardens: A Possible Contemporary Berlin

Text: Steffan Robel & Laura Veronese

A garden is by definition a planned and gated space: the word "garden" itself refers to an enclosure or compound, from the Old High German gart, cognate with "yard" in modern English[1].

The enclosure has been a central theme in the idea of the garden, including ancient Roman courtyards, which were surrounded by the house, as well as Chinese and Korean courtyard gardens and Japanese rock gardens. Over the course of its history, the garden has been seen as a precious oasis, protected from the potentially dangerous environment outside it – the wild world made by uncontrolled nature. It could then be said that the garden is defined by the limits between itself and its surroundings. In this understanding, the garden forms a counter-world to the one outside it. More recently the garden has been considered an antidote to urbanity, a peaceful spot of nature amid the ferocity of the contemporary urban landscape.

Thus, by questioning its boundaries, the un-gated community garden is reinterpreting the idea of the enclosed garden.

Recent decades have an increasing awareness of the role of green, public and un-gated spaces in the city. Community gardens have long been understood to improve psychological wellbeing and social interaction, to facilitate healing and to supplement supplies of fresh produce[2].

This paper will place particular emphasis on the idea of reinforcing social behavior through the practice of gardening, as well as on the relation between urban gardening and the self-image of Berlin.

These forms of urban gardens clearly extend beyond the common wish to increase the city's stock of green and natural terrain. These are spaces where food can grow and neighbors can interact while providing a place to share civic identity.

All the stuff is made of discarded furniture

Due to its extraordinary amount of vacant spaces, Berlin has a rich variety of un-gated community gardens, rendering the city an interesting case study. The city has been prolific in offering spaces for temporary use, hence fomenting bottom-up processes.

Research commissioned in 2004 by the Berlin Senate identified several temporary leisure, entertainment, social, sport and gardening projects located on unused sites and buildings throughout the city. The wide range of temporary uses found in Berlin reflects the heterogeneous nature of their promoters: artists, community groups, volunteers and activists in search of autonomous space[3].

However, it is commonly known that, since the Fall of the Berlin Wall, many of these voids have been developed differently, in an effort to endow the urban fabric with new structures and to redefine social patterns. Several have been temporarily reused for a variety of functions or been converted into green areas, parks and community gardens.

This urban-regenerative energy – channeled mostly in bottom-up processes – has constructed a specific image of the city's open spaces as a common ground to share new civic identity. Since 2010 the ideas for open spaces, such as "temporary" and "uncertain," have created such a strong aesthetic for the city that it can be counted as asset of its inhabitants.

Let us consider more deeply the phenomenon of urban gardening, which became quite a popular practice judging by the heterogeneous social pattern in some districts and neighborhoods.

As previously mentioned, Berlin possesses a large variety of mutually "cultivated" areas. These spaces are often considered commons: intercultural gardens, community gardens, guerilla gardens, school gardens, roof gardens and so on. They stir key questions about urban society, particularly with respect to social, cultural and biological diversity, participative urban design, ecology, education, integration and civic engagement.

Let us briefly explore a fascinating case study: the Allmende-Kontor community garden, located on the site of Berlin's former Tempelhof Airport. Tempelhof has a rich history: it was the airfield the western allies used to supply Berlin as the city was blockaded by the Soviets in 1948. The former airport, now known as "Tempelhofer Field" or "Tempelhofer Freedom," is 386 hectares, larger than New York's Central Park.

The airport was decommissioned in 2008, leaving an enormous space in the middle of the city, enclosed by fences and used by no one. After much criticism led by citizens demanding to use the huge open space left by the airport, it was opened to the public in 2010 while awaiting a future purpose.

photos © Stefania Facco

Photo of Allmende-Kontor community garden

The responsible authorities made possible a controlled use of Tempelhofer Field for the "meantime." The site of the closed airport was equipped with a minimum of facilities before opening it to the public. Ordinary citizens had the opportunity to submit project proposals and initiatives that could temporarily benefit from the site. Overnight, Tempelhofer Field became an extraordinary location for both citizens and visitors.

One of these initiatives is the Allmende-Kontor[4], an un-gated urban garden begun in 2011 as an intercultural community garden project. Like other projects at Tempelhofer Field, it is an initiative of citizens' willing to create a community dimension to life in the contemporary city.

In the Allmende-Kontor community garden, people from different cultural backgrounds grow plants and food in wooden containers, discarded furniture and in old sinks, instilling the garden with a specifically defined aesthetic quality. In summer it becomes a wonderful place to enjoy the sun; you can easily lose your orientation here, and feel as if you are in a re-interpreted countryside. The Allmende-Kontor underscores an important political dimension of urban gardening: simple social interactions slowly transform fixed spaces, building an alternative to the dominant order based on market logic[5].

Tempelhofer Field is open to everyone while the Allmende-Kontor has no fences: each day hundreds of people, visitors, tourists and passersby come to the garden. They cross it, walk by it or stroll through the planting beds. There is no claim of stolen fruit and vegetables or any other act of vandalism, revealing a respectful sense of "common."

This relationship between people from different cultures and the simple fact of cultivating soil in an urban lot generates forces that have a strong effect on the shape and use of the city.

It must be considered that urban gardening is perhaps the most explicit appropriation of wasteland or vacant space in order to promote an alternative way to live in the city.

Another relevant case study worthy of note is "Prinzessinnengarten" (Princess Gardens)[6] in Berlin. It is an un-gated, urban vegetable garden begun as a pilot project in 2009 in the center of the vibrant district of Kreuzberg. It is located at Moritzplatz, which, despite its prominent location at Berlin's geographical center, has been an abandoned and forgotten square for some decades. After the department store located here burned down in World War II, the square became an urban void until 2009.

Prinzessinnengarten is a mobile garden of transportable vegetable plots, consisting of locally produced vegetables raised in compost beds without using artificial substances. Especially in spring, when it wakes after winter, the garden reveals the true beauty of vegetables, sprouts and fruit. The garden has a cafe selling products from the garden, such as juices and soups. Patrons can sit in the shade of the still young birch trees near the cafe and enjoy an organic meal made from the garden's produce. It is a small piece of calm in the city: the noises of Berlin sound faraway, even though the garden is sited in a very dense and urbanized part of the city. This garden shows how small-scale intervention can stimulate active citizenship in a local neighborhood, and how it can work as a motor to further initiatives. A utopia of new urban dream weavers knitting communities together, to work and relax, to discuss and share, to learn and digest the fruits of their own labor. As moral support to all the urban farmers of the world, this simple and powerful project was recently granted the Jury and Public Prize at the 2010 Utopia Awards.

It is clear that civil society is increasingly recognizing and supporting the socially integrative power of urban agriculture. In the city of Berlin, recruits of "urban pioneers" were set to make possible the temporary use of wasteland. Urban gardens can thus be seen as a stimulus for greater community involvement among residents aiming to make contemporary cities friendlier and better places to live.

Photos of "Prinzessinnengarten" (Princess Gardens)

1. Gilles Clément, Une brève histoire du jardin, ditions JC Béhar, Paris 2011 (in English: A Brief History of the Garden)
2. Donna Armstrong, A survey of community gardens in upstate New York: Implications for health promotion and community development in Health & Place 6 (2000) 319 - 327. See also Hynes, 1996; Murphy, 1991
3. Ref, Urban catalyst 2003, in Staging the New Berlin, p. 241
4. The German word "Allmende" can be translated into English as "common." The term

Allmende originated in the Middle Ages as al(ge)meinde, almeine or almeide, meaning "common pasture," and describes land held by a village community, a real property within a local district.
5. Karin Werner, Eigensinnige Beheimatungen. Gemeinschaftsgärten als Orte des Widerstandes gegen die neoliberale Ordnung. In: Müller, Christa pp. 54-75.
6. see http://prinzessinnengarten.net/ and the monograph Nomadisch Grün, Prinzessinnengärten. Anders gärtnern in der Stadt, Dumont Buchverlag, 2012

Steffan Robel

Steffan Robel, born in Pirmasens, Germany in 1972, is founder and executive director of A24 Landschaft. Robel studied landscape architecture at TU Berlin and at the Internationale Agrarische Hogeschool Larenstein in The Netherlands, as well as construction management in Weimar. He held various posts before creating A24 Landschaft in 2005. Robel worked as an instructor, teaching courses at HafenCity University Hamburg and at Hochschule Anhalt. His designs have won awards both in Germany and abroad; he has been a competition juror since 2006.

Laura Veronese

Laura Veronese is a Berlin-based architect and holds a Masters in Architecture and Urbanism from IUAV, University of Venice, Italy. Her work mainly explores concepts of natural places in contemporary urban landscapes, green mobility, temporary spaces, processes concerning physical and social transformations in urban areas. She is currently working on her PhD dissertation at the IUAV University.

Her last article " Brand-Urban-Landscapes: the Transformation of Open Spaces in Berlin" was presented in Paris at U&U Symposium in October 2013.

She has collaborated with several landscape- and urban planning offices. Laura Veronese is currently working at the landscape architecture office A24Landschaft in Berlin.

Photograph provided by Martin Arfalk

A New Version of Community Garden: An Intimate Character and a Personalized Design

Text: Martin Arfalk

Traditionally we have built squares in our cities and gardens in our homes. The public and private life has been regarded as two different spaces in our city society. One is designed as a meeting place for everyone while the other one is a private room for the individual. Today, a number of hybrid spaces have emerged as the lines between public and private space have blurred. Within this spectrum, we find the community garden. It is a space open to be experienced by the public but only acted upon by those individuals with a stake in the community. The resulting gardens are typically defined by their high quality, their community engagement, and their carefulness. For me, the hybrid nature and the carefulness of the resulting community gardens have become an inspiration to how we plan, design and handle the development of new public squares. In today's environment of professional practice, discussions of the different public and private interests many times merge into one, which I believe is generating a new version of the community garden: the public space with an intimate character and a personalized design.

The public square is traditionally the place of freedom, a place where a person can act on the behalf of other people. The public square is an open source platform and a meeting point that invites everyone. It is a neutral space in our city and we fight to protect our public spaces from commercialization and privatization (as city centers move or the demand of space changes). Over time the role of public squares has varied and its right of existing has sometimes been disputed in the modernization of our cities. However, in the last years the understanding of the importance of the public space has grown. This has been shown in the example of the pedestrianization of Times Square in New York. Successful projects have helped create a growing attitude that public squares need to remain a strong part of our society and become living rooms for its citizens. This adds new perspectives which need to be taken into account when designing our new squares today, namely, the merging of public and private interest within the square. Furthermore, we demand the spaces between the buildings become performative surfaces: absorbing and storing water, providing green to answer recreational desires, and allowing flexibility over time.

The ambition to combine public and private interest within a square has come forward in two projects that I've worked on in the last ten years. The first project is Leonardo da Vinci Square in Meerwijk Haarlem, The Netherlands and the other is Hermods Square in Malmö, Sweden. In these two examples the common driving force has been a public, community square with the intention to create a living room for the local community. Both squares are located on the outskirts of the main public network of the larger city (Haarlem and Malmö) and function as key meeting places within the neighborhood. The first example, Leonardo da Vinci Square was created on a new, artificial island. The square grabs the two sides of the water with two bridges that emerge from the surface of the square to become sitting benches. On one side the square neighbors a school and on the other a shopping market and housing. In the design, the neighboring programs are invited to take part in the life of the square and visitors are invited to use a number of small, specific landscapes where form and function are integrated. The square has its own identifiable character with pine trees and a glittering nature stone surface. Unique elements, such as the stairs from the parking garage, have been designed with a sloping roof that invites the local school children to play. The carefulness of the design is handled as if it was a garden as materials, such as wooden benches, soft shapes and trees, were chosen to create an intimate atmosphere. Over time, Leonardo da Vinci Square has become a public space with a strongly personalized design and a community feeling within a traditional, small town.

Achieving a similar intimate atmosphere Hermods Square is a different take on the square as community garden. Like Leonardo da Vinci Square, the design closely integrates function and form. However, where all aspects in the Leonardo da Vinci Square are incapsulated into the designed shapes the design in Hermods Square aims to create a framework for the content of the square. The design inspiration came from the fragmentary nature of the flintstone found in the surrounding landscape and the design connects across the bisecting street to form a unified square that prioritizes pedestrian flow and creates a cohesive design language. The resulting design creates a series of rooms, called fragments, which tie together the old village structure with the newly developed residential area. These rooms are filled with plants, play areas, resting areas and areas for walking and biking. Hermods Square is a community platform for initiatives. Entrances to the adjacent houses bring life to the square and local residents can express their private interests on their front steps. As time passes the idea is that the square's flexibility will allow for the design to follow new demands and initiatives that grow from the personal expression of the neighborhood.

One of the most important words in design is carefulness. This is often determined by the size of a project, the cultural context and the understanding from the client. We have, as designers, an important role

Photograph provided by David Dudzik

to debate a particular design, its role and purpose, and we need to argue to find ways to personalize places in our cities, in order to create spaces people want to take care of, visit and make even better. The 8th Biennial of Landscape Architecture in Barcelona is exploring this in this year's theme "A Landscape for You." The biennial in September wants to discuss what should be the landscape design and planning nowadays, aiming to provide a plausible (and exciting) future. The exploration of what the community garden is and can become, understanding its new role in the city is therefore a highly present topic. Inspiring challenges are ahead.

Martin Arfalk

Martin Arfalk, born 1974 in Sweden, is the founder of Mandaworks, a landscape architect and urban design company in Stockholm, Sweden and Shanghai, China. Martin Arfalk has several years of international experience. He has participated in several award-winning projects and his strength ranges from conception to completion. The international profile of the company creates an important added value to the company's work. The company combines the design process and a careful mapping of the data with a willingness to develop special qualities. Beside his work at Mandaworks, Martin currently runs the advanced design studio, Sustainable Urban Dynamics, within the master's program of Sustainable Urban Design at the School of Architecture in Lund, Sweden.

Lake extension, bridge and fountains designed by LDA Design. Image courtesy of Southwark Council

New Design Transforms Burgess Park

Text: B. Cannon Ivers

Burgess Park is a story of cultural evolution and urban transformation. In the 19th and early 20th century, the site that is now Burgess Park was a dense industrial area of London with warehouses, factories and residential areas defining the boundary of the site. The Grand Surrey Canal was an important asset of the industrial engine of the site and ran the full length of the site for nearly 1.5 kilometers.

In 1943, the Abercrombie Plan was developed for the post WWII re-planning of London and the industrial site that is now Burgess Park was identified as a strategic area to be converted to open space to act as a significant park for southeast London. During the War, more than 70 bombs fell on the Burgess Park site, augmenting the transformation of the site from dense industry to an urban park. Over the next 40 years, the site was systematically cleared and overtime converted to the London Borough of Southwark's largest park covering 51 hectares. However, a comprehensive masterplan was never developed for the park, which resulted in a park that

evolved incrementally and in an ad-hoc way as and when funding became available. Demolished buildings were spread across the site and covered with soil, onto which trees were planted, establishing a site topography and tree groupings that would later define the disjointed structure of the park.

LDA Design became part of the Burgess Park story in 2009 after winning an international design competition that drew the interest of more than 100 landscape practices from around the world. The scale and location of Burgess Park made it one of the last great London parks to undergo such a dramatic transformation, which was an aspect that appealed to design practices. Large-scale change was already underway in this part of London as the adjacent Aylesbury Estate, one of the largest social housing developments in London, began the 20-year process of regeneration.

The LDA Design team began the process of working with the community to understand the needs and desires of the various user groups. With more than

Park entrance designed by LDA Design. Image courtesy of B. Cannon Ivers

100 languages spoken in this ethically rich area, the public consultation process quickly became an integral aspect of how the park would be revitalized. Over 27 consultation events took place, reaching more than 1,000 people in the adjacent neighborhoods. The process crystallized the needs and desires of the community and the design team incorporated these aspirations into the masterplan.

The fundamental issue of the park was its lack of structure and cohesion, which in turn led to an eroded sense of park identity and community safety. The incremental development of the park led to a series of disparate landforms that limited how the park could be connected, how it was perceived and understood, and most importantly, how people used the park. LDA proposed a series of significant structural design moves, overlaid with valuable cultural facilities and community-led projects. The first structural design move was a dramatic reshaping of the existing landforms by sculpting more than 90,000m³ of soil; enough to fill the Turbine Hall of the Tate Modern in London. The new landforms, reaching 7 meters in height, create a recognizable structure for the park, provide unexpected compositions and increase the usability of the park. The sculpted landforms also signal key entrances, frame vistas and give structure to the new footpaths that connect park to the wider communities. Most noticeably, perhaps, is how the re-imagined landforms make the park feel larger, more ample and able to accommodate the myriad user groups. Once the structure of the park had been established with new landforms and rationalized

footpaths that take people where they want to go, the design team focused on the provision of key facilities and establishing an identity for the park.

The two main entrances provide the first impression and set the standard for the rest of the park. Inspired by the fascinating industrial heritage of the park, large architectural screens, measuring 3.5 meters × 13 meters in length, showcase the historic road layout of the park in a stylized and unique way. These iconic elements give the design an undeniable sense of place and a strong identity for the park. Coupled with the screens, are bold archways that frame the entrance landscape and create legible entrance points. Each entrance provides a sustainable "rain garden" that captures surface water drainage and creates a diverse planting typology. The planting includes species that can tolerate periods of standing water and dry spells when rain water is in short supply.

Vandalism and anti-social behavior was a real issue for the park. The lack of play provision and other activities for young people in the park contributed to the vandalism of the park because vandals were often fuelled by boredom. To combat this issue, LDA Design created a cutting-edge and colorful play area for older children and teenagers. The notion of imaginative play underpins the design by creating an undulating landscape onto which stand-alone play components are overlaid. The undulations are accentuated with simple white lining that pulls the play space together as a unified whole, doubling as "sprinter lanes." The design intent was to align with the reality that children like to create their own play experiences and the play space would give them the freedom to do that. The linchpin of the play space is a 15-meter-long slide that tunnels through the 6-meter-high landform, often with queues of children waiting for their chance to speed down the slide. In addition to the play area, LDA Design delivered a competition standard BMX track with specialist contractors Clark and Kent. This facility provides a training ground for the British Olympic hopefuls and national champions, whilst also enabling the younger generation to get a taste of the adrenaline-charged sport.

Biodiversity and horticulture were key drivers and community aspirations for the park from the outset. Working with ecologist and Professor James Hitchmough from Sheffield University, the design team created seven new habitats, including wet woodlands, marginal planting, signature meadows and ornamental planting, whilst converting amenity grass areas to species-rich lawns. The scale of intervention on a park of 51 hectares demanded that the design team think laterally about how to establish new habitats and attractive horticulture displays. James's extensive knowledge of plant communities has led him to become the foremost specialist in the establishment of large areas of planting from seeds. Once the sculptural landforms had been defined on site, 30,000m^2 of Burgess Park was sown with bespoke seed mixes devised by Professor Hitchmough. The horticultural displays have become one of the talking points, creating a sense of social pride and community ownership.

During the design process of phase 1 of the project, LDA Design was commissioned to develop a long-term vision for the park and design a masterplan that could be delivered over a number of phases. The masterplan was driven by the concept of "Elegant Sufficiency;" a term relates to a state of completeness. Burgess Park has never been finished; it's a work in progress and the masterplan points to a condition in which it can finally be regarded as mature and complete. The term also refers to a point in time when the park starts to play a more complete role in people's lives – where it has developed a programmatic diversity that allows it to appeal to everyone.

Entrance rain gardens and seasonal planting displays designed by LDA Design and James Hitchmough. Image courtesy of B. Cannon Ivers

One of the drivers of this programmatic diversity will undoubtedly be climate change. It is widely acknowledged that winters are going to become increasingly wet with higher incidences of storm events and that summers will become longer, drier and hotter. In response to increased storm events the park will be expected to integrate a responsible approach to water management where water is captured and stored for when it is needed in the dry months, rather than simply being discharged into the surface water drainage system. As food prices rise the notion of growing one's own food will become increasingly popular and there will be pressure on the park to integrate areas of community food growing as well as food for free. The park will become increasingly important as a habitat for wildlife and will incorporate new types of habitat driven by the prospect of a dry future. The park will not only adapt to climate change but will also try to mitigate the impacts of it.

In summary, Vitruvius the Roman writer, architect and engineer famously wrote, "Well building and design hath three conditions: firmness, commodity and delight." True to this dictum, the park will provide a firmness in the topography, footpaths and entrance; commodity in the form of the play area, event space, BMX track, outdoor gym and trails, community growing areas; delight in the gardens, the lake, woodlands and enriched biodiversity across the site.

B. Cannon Ivers

B. Cannon Ivers is an associate with LDA Design and a Chartered Member of the Landscape Institute. He brings a creative, conceptual design specialism to LDA Design's London Office. His work is driven by three-dimensional design and analysis, resulting in contemporary and responsive design solutions to the constraints and strengths that exist within a site. Cannon has a rich appreciation of the importance of site-specific characteristics and strives to create sympathetic and complementary design solutions.

LDA Design is an independent, design, environment and sustainability consultancy. Established for over 30 years with a professional team of over 120 people, they work in the UK and internationally and equally, for the private and public sector.

Create Comfortable High-quality Community Spaces

– An Interview with G&C Architects

Martin González Cavia, Marta González Cavia & Jorge Cabrera Bartolomé

G&C Arquitectos, founded in 1997, is an architectural firm which specializes in architecture, urban planning, and landscaping.

Some of its standout projects include designing and landscaping the Bake Eder parcel, Zelaieta Park, Herriko Square and its surroundings in Amorebieta-Etxano, and Atalaya Park in Armintza, Lemoiz, all of which were the result of public design competitions.

They recently won, in conjunction with JDVDP Architects, the Zorrozaurre green areas and outdoor spaces competition in Bilbao which was based on the masterplan of Zaha Hadid.

Their professional development has been focused on landscaping, urban renewal, and both civic and corporate architecture. The G&C Arquitectos team is comprised of founders Marta González Cavia, Martin González Cavia, and Jorge Cabrera Bartolomé.

What in your opinion are community gardens?

First and foremost, they are spaces meant to improve the quality of life in urban settings. They serve a variety of purposes, the most important of which is creating an environment that provides members with opportunity to interact.

In your mind, what is the most important part when designing community gardens?

Two things: the site and its users. The key to designing is understanding not just the physical layout of a place, but also its social and cultural context, that is to say how it has been used and how it can be used.

The development of urban public spaces and community gardens projects aims to meet diverse needs of society. We are speaking of how important user is in the development of a good design.

When dealing with community gardens, could you please tell us what factors we should pay special attention to? Sustainable features?

In the initial analysis, we pay special attention to the history of the site, the topography, the urban scale and the acoustic and weather conditions – including wind, water and sun.

All of these come into play in the designing phase when we focus on accessibility, what vegetation best suits the environment, appropriate materials and lighting, or in short, the urban landscape and how the garden is connected to its surroundings and the rest of the city.

Bioclimatic considerations are always the foundation for our sustainable designs, but we also integrate key technologies to maximize energy efficiency.

Another essential aspect of planning any garden is thoroughly analyzing and understanding the water cycle of each particular location and how to use it sustainably. This requires knowing the average rainfall, the climatological conditions (temperature, relative humidity, and orientation), the capacity for evaporation and transpiration of the soil and the chosen plant and vegetation varieties.

The integrated water management includes green roof technology for filtration, rain water harvesting in cisterns, bio-swales, filter and infiltration systems and open and closed storage.

Does sustainability of a community garden play an important role in city environment? In what ways?

We cannot exaggerate the importance of a community garden in a city – by creating a green space in what is otherwise a sea of concrete, you provide members of that community with a place to escape the noise and the rush of the city while giving them the opportunity to interact on a daily basis – something that is otherwise unlikely.

It's necessary to reconsider the areas in which our life takes place, our urban space and landscape. It is important to think about the time spent by our neighbors, our older relatives, our children and ourselves in these types of places, and how we spend our free time (leisure, sports, games and social relations).

There is a general demand for a greater awareness of sustainability that is forcing us to bring about a change that will improve people's quality of life and these public relationships we are speaking about.

In the area of sustainability designers have to make significant effort in terms of design resources.

What is your inspiration or concept idea when dealing with projects?

Each project is different, but they all start the same way, with a deep analysis of the site. Inspiration may come from understanding the history or from solving the perceived problems of a site, or from the location itself… It is never the same twice.

How could you help your clients to maximize the design budget?

The best community gardens don't have to be the most expensive space: the cost does not dictate the quality of a space.

The designer has to adapt to whatever budget constraints a client may have. However, one might consider undertaking dramatic changes in phases.

In your mind, what are the opportunities and challenges when designing community gardens?

Each project is both an opportunity and a challenge in and of itself. We are always aware that intervening in public spaces can improve the quality of life of many people.

What are connections among community gardens, architecture and people?

They can't be separated: the architecture, the

spaces they create and people who work, live and use those spaces form a whole.

It's very important that people, the users, participate in the initial design process by contributing their own ideas.

This requires a team of experts to lead a coordinated effort to elicit their participation, with the support of architects and landscape architects.

By giving citizens a greater role in the development process, you give more value to their connection with space.

What are the criteria in designing community gardens?

The most important factors to take into consideration when designing comfortable high-quality public spaces are:

Thermal comfort
With a focus on improving the comfort level within spaces by guaranteeing that sun exposure is neither excessive nor inadequate, controlling wind through the use of filters or barriers; the appropriate selection of materials – depending on the intensity of the color a space can be warmed or cooled.

Acoustic conditions
The frequent presence of nearby traffic means that the acoustic comfort must be another objective in the design of community gardens. There are diverse options for acoustic protection that can be integrated into the design, and many

of these come from natural sources like anti-noise barriers, plant filters, a sloping topography, or sound-absorbent flooring.

Perception of security
How do we improve perception of security? By increasing the visibility and transparency of a space we foster the natural protection that can be provided by citizens. This aspect is most important for children and the elderly, the most vulnerable members of a community.

Lighting
It is also important to understand that lighting projects are absolutely essential to help us create a light map that is more in tune with our idea of

space in each project.

When approaching a lighting project we have in our hands a "material" that allows us to define and to communicate spaces both objectively and subjectively.

A lighting system should work at different heights depending on the different requirements of the project, and its aesthetic value should contribute to the configuration of the space and to the image of the site.

Vegetation
Vegetation is one of the basic components of community gardens, to allow creating artistic

landscape experiences that recognize the diversity of scale and wonderful contrasts.

In the future, would you think community gardens will be popularized? Why?

Without a doubt. Community gardens are a necessity; they have always been considered socially important. They generate a kind of public life that allows members of a community to interact in and take ownership of that space, which in turn has the power to change their very perception of their community.

Sew Back the Urban Fabric and Adapt to Neighbors' Requirements
– An Interview with Pol Femenias

Pol Femenias

Pol Femenias Arquitectes (PFA), Barcelona, Spain is based on a wide vision on architectural design, working from its early conceptual design to the details of the finished construction.

PFA understand their design as a research for wellness of the user, trying hard to create spaces that give comfort. They are convinced that architecture must not be a final goal, but a means to facilitate relationships.

Though being a young firm, they had the chance to work on very different types of projects, from the large-scale urban planning, housing projects and interior design, to the simplest detail of furniture design. In all of them they try to solve with simplicity the complexity that carries any creative process, always keeping refinement, rigor and emotion on each step of the way.

PFA was founded in 2010. Through these years they have gained the trust of both public and private clients from all around the world, and were awarded for their works (ASCER Award 2014).

What do you think is a community garden?

I understand it's the public space we all share, with emphasis on the treatment of the surfaces as to hold vegetation, opposed to those urban spaces that need to be more "hard" due to the use they have.

Do we need a topic before designing it?

Of course. As in any project, the design of a space, whether it's indoor or outdoor, as a place that will be lived, it should have a purpose, an idea that holds it together. Each garden should be designed according to its surroundings, to its climate, and to the kind of people that will enjoy it.

What does it need on the natural environment?

The public gardens need to be sustainable, understood as that they need to be conceived and designed so that they are easy to keep. That can only be achieved by adapting each design to the particular properties of the site.

In your mind, what is the most important part when designing

community gardens?

Thinking how it will be lived, how people will enjoy that space. I try hard to guess in early phases of the design, what are the needs of the people who will use that garden. All the design comes from those needs and tries to adapt to those requirements.

What are the criteria in designing community gardens?

It depends on many factors. For example, one factor could be the orientation of that space, how does the sun affect on the garden, which areas will be shaded most of the time during the day and which ones will be more exposed. Depending on the city of the world, you will seek for comfortable places protected from the sun, as happens in our projects in southern Europe. In cold countries happens the opposite. That would be just one factor, but there are lots of them that make a good design: relation with the city, choice of species, proportions, etc…

What is your inspiration or concept idea when dealing with projects?

Each project is different. In Sant Feliu we were deeply inspired by the surroundings, and the void we had to deal with. The demolition of the old factory left a wound in the city, and our design put the effort in trying to sew back the urban fabric. All the project is based on that idea and the structure of the garden follows the pattern left by the existing houses that surround the gardens. The treatment of the wall was also inspired by that. We didn't want to make tabula rasa with the place and tried to capture all the complexity it had on the first place. I think it's been a complete success, as all the neighbors love the result.

When dealing with community gardens, could you please tell us what factors we should pay special attention to? Sustainable features?

One factor that always works for me to see if a public space is well designed is to look if there are people using it. You can have the best garden, with beautiful trees and incredible architecture around it, but if people don't feel comfortable in it, if they feel to be outsiders in that place, then you have failed. The clue in designing public space is thinking on people, trying to make them comfortable. Once you get that, you can put your effort on other things.

Does sustainability of a community garden play an important role in city environment? In what ways?

In the bottom line, a community garden is paid by all of us with our taxes. In the same way we don't want to buy a car that consumes lots of fuel and generates contamination, we should be proud of the public buildings and spaces that are thought so that they don't consume much energy no neither its construction nor its maintenance. In that way, sustainability plays a crucial role on the design.

What kind of plants do designers usually use? Why?

Once again, each project has its own demands. In the matter of species, we architects always work with botanical specialists to give us advice on which are the appropriate plants for a site. The design has to go along with the maintenance, as gardens are not finished after three or four years, when all the species are fully grown.

People in different ages have their own preferences for sports facilities. How do you deal with that?

Sports facilities must be adapted to a certain age, and that affects, for example, the materials they are made of. Facilities for kids are often made of soft materials, so they don't get hurt, and so is the pavement. Sports facilities for teenagers, on one hand, are focused more on the adventure of the freedom of choice, on making them feel independent and owner of their own decisions, with layouts that include multiple activities in the same pace. On the other hand, sports facilities for the elder focus more on a single exercise.

Would you talk about pathway design in detail? Is there any requirement for degree of slope or special materials, for example?

A project is fully enjoyed once you've been able to walk through it. That's when you really feel the atmosphere, the smells, the shadows. We often tend to analyze a design only based on photographs or drawings, and that makes it difficult to fully understand some things like, the slope the project had to deal with. Sometimes the slope can affect the whole design and be the reason of most of the choices made in the project. That cannot always be seen looking at the photographs. We are incredibly sensible to slopes. All cities have a minimum 1-2% slope and we don't even notice it. However, things change when that turns to 4-5%. You have to bear in mind that if you design a pathway with a 7-8% slope, people will surely look for another way around, as its really uncomfortable.

For the bench, does it have to need a back? Why?

In my opinion, they basically need to be comfortable. You can find lots of bench with back which are not well designed, and often the slope of the back is not appropriate or is made with the wrong material. A bench with no back is probably easier to design and can be used in different ways, as the back clearly points how a bench should be used, but again, if the bench is comfortable and user-friendly, it doesn't matter if it has back or not.

What do you think about the future of community gardens?

I think that we designers have the opportunity to bring people back to design with community gardens, as they as no other are projects that will be used not by the inhabitant of a house or the worker of an office building, but by people of all ages, races and ideologies. That makes it design for people, as they are the final users. Making people the center of the design is what will guide the future of public space design.

Would you like to share some experience with other architects?

We architects are all inspired by the work of others, and as I want to be thankful for all I've learned from the experiences shared by other colleagues, I'd be glad if my experience would be of any use to any architect.